I.O.O.F. Digest of the Laws of the Independent Order of Odd-fellows

John R Wiltsie
Newburgh
March 4th
AD 1848

I. O. O. F.

DIGEST OF THE LAWS

OF THE

INDEPENDENT ORDER

OF

ODD-FELLOWS:

TO WHICH IS ADDED AN

APPENDIX,

CONTAINING THE

CONSTITUTION, LAWS AND RULES OF ORDER,

ALL NECESSARY FORMS AND THE FUNERAL CEREMONY:

PREPARED BY THE FOLLOWING COMMITTEE, APPOINTED BY GRAND
SIRE SHERLOCK, AT THE COMMUNICATION OF 1846:

JAMES L. RIDGELY, HOWELL HOPKINS, ROBERT H.
GRIFFIN, WILLIAM E. PARMENTER.

Published by order of the Grand Lodge of the United States.

PHILADELPHIA:

PRINTED BY JOHN H. GIHON,

CORNER OF SIXTH AND CHESNUT STS.

....

1848.

CONTENTS.

To the R. W. Grand Lodge of the United States:

The Special Committee appointed at the last communication to prepare a Digest of the Laws of the Order, respectfully submit the following report:

The committee have devoted to the subject their undivided attention during a long session, and have endeavored by diligent labor to comply with the terms of the resolution under which they were appointed. They have examined thoroughly, and with great care, all the printed proceedings of the Grand Lodge, and have extracted every thing in the form of well settled law, which they could discover. They have frequently been embarrassed by conflicting decisions, but in all such cases they have either guided themselves by the weight of authority, or, where the preponderance was doubtful, have sought light from general and unquestioned principles. They have occasionally found it necessary to fill up spaces which the recorded legislation had left vacant, but they have introduced nothing to supply such defects which has not been sanctioned by well ascertained usage. In rare instances also they have felt constrained to incorporate into their work decisions which have been departed from by later legislation, but they have always yielded to the necessity with great reluctance, and only when they were convinced that such a course was indispensable to the preservation of the unity and harmony of the system. Amid such masses of laws as have passed under their review, it was impossible that there should be entire consistency, but the committee have been extremely gratified to find that the instances of deviation from the true line have presented themselves at very wide intervals.

The plan which the committee have adopted, they hope will approve itself to the judgment of the Grand Lodge. After due deliberation, it was selected as the one best calculated for convenience of reference, and as affording the fairest opportunity of compressing the work into limits sufficiently narrow. It has been an object of which the committee have never lost sight, to avoid all unnecessary repetition, in order that the fraternity might be furnished with a hand book, containing all that was essential, but at the same time not repulsive by reason of prolixity. To accomplish this, they have labored care-

3

fully, but they have never sacrificed to this idea of convenience any thing which they deemed of importance.

The Digest is accompanied by an Appendix containing all the *forms* which have been sanctioned, or are necessary under the laws, and also a revised copy of the Constitution, Laws, and Rules of Order, into which are incorporated the amendments from time to time adopted. In the preparation of this latter portion of the appendix, some verbal alterations have been found absolutely necessary, but in no instance has the sense been interfered with.

The committee now ask leave to surrender their work into the hands of this Grand Lodge. It has been their constant care during many days and nights of labor, and they part from it with deep anxiety, that it should be acceptible to the body under whose directions it has been executed.

> JAMES L. RIDGELY,
> HOWELL HOPKINS,
> ROBERT H. GRIFFIN,
> WM. E. PARMENTER.

DIGEST OF THE LAWS OF THE ORDER.

DIVISION FIRST.

GRAND LODGE OF THE UNITED STATES.

ARTICLE I.

ITS COMPOSITION, POWERS AND JURISDICTION.

§1. The R. W. Grand Lodge of the United States, of the Independent Order of Odd-Fellows, is composed of Officers, Representatives and Past Grand Sires.—(*Cons. Arts. II & VII.*)

§2. It is the fountain of all true and legitimate authority in Odd-Fellowship.—(*Cons. Art. I, Jour. vol.* 1, *p.* 537, 543–4, *et vide vol.* 2, *p.* 86.)

§3. It has exclusive power to make, alter and regulate the work, language and regalia of the Order; to pass general laws for the government of the fraternity in all its branches; and to declare the usages and customs of the Order.—(*Cons. Art. I.*)

§4. It has exclusive power to create Grand and Subordinate Lodges, and Grand and Subordinate Encampments, in any part of the world, delegating to such bodies so much of its authority as it may deem proper.—(*Cons. Art. I, vol.* 1, *p.* 537, 544.)

§5. It has full power to recall or annul any charter, warrant or dispensation issued by its authority; and no Lodge or Encampment, Grand or Subordinate, can lawfully exist without its continued sanction and approval.—(*Journal, passim.*)

§6. It has power to superintend the work of the Order, in all its branches; to enforce the usages and general laws

9

of the Order ; and to punish for non-conformity thereto.—
(Cons. Art. I, Journal, passim.)

§7. By an act of incorporation passed at the December
session, 1841, of the General Assembly of Maryland, it has
corporate powers, with the provision, however, "that the
said corporation or body politic shall not at any time hold
or possess property, real, personal, or mixed, exceeding in
annual value the sum of twenty thousand dollars."—*(Vol.
1, p. xi.)*

§8. It is the supreme and ultimate tribunal to which con-
troversies and disputes in the Order may be referred:—
(Cons. Art. I.)

§9. It will entertain jurisdiction of an appeal by an individual member from the judgment of his Subordinate Lodge
or Encampment, working immediately under its jurisdiction,
and of charges preferred against such a Lodge or Encampment by a member.—*(Vol. 1, p. 80, 91-2 ; opinion of
Grand Sire, approved by Grand Lodge, letters of 1845,
No. 86.)*

§10. It will entertain jurisdiction of an appeal by an individual member of a Grand Lodge or Grand Encampment
from a judgment of expulsion, the result of proceedings
originally commenced against him on the floor of said
Grand Lodge.—*(Deduction from general principles.)*

§11. It will entertain jurisdiction of an appeal by a mi-
nority of a Grand Lodge or Grand Encampment from the
decision of a majority thereof on any question of general
importance.—*(Vol. 1, p. 179, 275, 480, 547, vol. 2. p.
326-7.)*

§12. It will entertain jurisdiction of an appeal by an
expelled Lodge or Encampment from the judgment of expulsion pronounced by its immediate superior ; provided,
the subordinate has submittted and surrendered its effects.
—*(Cons. Art. I, as amended, vol. 2, p. 145.)*

§13. It will not entertain jurisdiction of any other case
unless presented by a Grand Lodge or Grand Encampment,
or with the consent and express sanction of the one or the
other.—*Cons. Art. I, vol. 1, p. 36, 130, 238-9, 282, 347.)*

ARTICLE II.—Grand Officers.

§1. The elective officers are the M. W. Grand Sire, R. W. Deputy Grand Sire, R. W. Grand Recording Secretary, R. W. Grand Corresponding Secretary, and R. W. Grand Treasurer.—*(Cons. Art. III.)*

§2. The appointed officers are the R. W. Grand Marshal, R. W. Grand Guardian, R. W. Grand Chaplain, and R. W. Grand Messenger.—*Cons. Art. III, and usage.)*

§3. The Grand Sire, Deputy Grand Sire, Grand Recording Secretary, and Grand Treasurer, are elected biennially at the stated meeting in September. The Grand Corresponding Secretary is elected and holds his office at the pleasure of the Grand Lodge.—*(Cons. Art. III.)*

§4. The elections take place by ballot on the second day of the session. The officers are nominated and elected separately, beginning with the Grand Sire and going regularly down. Pending an *election*, no new nomination can be received. Pending a *ballot*, no motion can be entertained, or debate or explanation permitted. No person, not regularly nominated, can be elected. Every ballot, whether blank or otherwise, is counted, and a majority of all the votes polled is necessary to a choice.—*(Rules of Order 12, 21, vol. 1, 309, vol. 2, 267, Cons. Arts. XIV & XV.)*

§5. Each Grand Lodge and each Grand Encampment, working under an unreclaimed warrant granted by the Grand Lodge of the United States, may by its representative (or representatives) nominate a candidate for the office of Grand Sire, and also a candidate for the office of Deputy Grand Sire.—*(Cons. Art. XIV.)*

§6. The candidates for Grand Sire and Deputy Grand Sire must be Past Grand Masters, of the R. P. Degree, and contributing members of Subordinate Lodges.—*(Cons. Art. XIV.)*

§7. Candidates for all other offices, elective or appointed, must be Past Grands of the R. P. Degree, and contributing members of Subordinate Lodges.—*(Usage.)*

§8. The appointed officers are nominated by the Grand Sire, subject to the approval of the Grand Lodge, and continue in office during the term of the Grand Sire appointing them, unless removed by him for cause.—*(Cons. Art. III.)*

§9. The officers are installed and enter on their duties at the stated meeting next ensuing the election. The installation takes place on the second day of the session.—*(Cons. Art. III, 12 Rule of Order.)*

§10. Should any of the officers elect fail to appear at the appointed time of installation, the particular office shall be declared vacant, the Grand Lodge shall proceed to a new election to fill the vacancy, and the officer so elected shall be accordingly installed.—*(Cons. Art. III.)*

§11. In case of the death, resignation, disqualification, or refusal to serve, of the Grand Sire, the duties of the office shall be performed by the Deputy Grand Sire until the next stated meeting of the Grand Lodge, when an election shall be had for Grand Sire. In case of the death, resignation, disqualification, or refusal to serve of any other officer, elective or appointed, the Grand Sire shall appoint some qualified brother to perform the duties of the vacant office until the next stated meeting, when an election or formal appointment, as the case may require, shall take place.—*(Cons. Art. XIII.)*

§12. In the absence of the Grand Sire and Deputy Grand Sire, the Grand Lodge shall elect a G. Sire *pro tempore.*—*(Cons. Art. V.)*

§13. All officers are required to attend each meeting of the Grand Lodge and perform such duties as are enjoined by the laws and regulations of the Order. All officers under the presiding officer are required to obey the directions of that officer.—*(Cons. Art. III.)*

§14. No officer (who is not also a representative) is permitted to vote, except the Grand Sire in case of equal division. No such officer is permitted to address the Grand Lodge, except upon leave first asked and obtained.—*(Cons. Art. X, vol. 1, 365.)*

§15. All necessary travelling expenses of the officers are paid out of the funds of the Grand Lodge.—*(Vol. 1, p. 115.)*

§16. Any officer may be re-elected or re-appointed.—*(Journal, passim.)*

ARTICLE III.—GRAND SIRE.

§1. The Grand Sire is required to preside at all meetings of the Grand Lodge, preserve order and enforce the laws thereof—to exercise, during the recess of the Grand Lodge, a general superintendence over the interests of the Order—to make a report at every stated meeting of his acts and doings in his office—to open or cause to be opened all Subordinate Lodges and Encampments receiving a warrant from the Grand Lodge of the United States, and to visit the same at least once a year, either personally or by deputy—to open or cause to be opened each Grand Lodge and Grand Encampment chartered by the Grand Lodge of the United States—to select and forward, through the Representatives at each regular session of the Grand Lodge, the T. P. W., and in case any particular jurisdiction is not represented to communicate the same by such other safe means as he may select, taking care that it be transmitted to all parts entitled to it so as to go into use on the first day of January in each and every year—to nominate the appointed officers of the Grand Lodge—to appoint all committees of the Grand Lodge, unless otherwise specially ordered—to give the casting vote whenever the Grand Lodge is equally divided—to sign all orders on the Treasurer authorized by a vote of the Grand Lodge—to decide all questions of Order in the Grand Lodge, subject to an appeal to the Grand Lodge—and to give advice and instruction, when called on, to the Grand and Subordinate Lodges and Encampments, working under the Grand Lodge of the United States, on all subjects connected with the Order, its laws, usages and customs.— (*Cons. Arts. III & IV; By-Laws, Arts. I, II, III, XIV, XVIII, XXVI; Rules of Order 26 and 33, and approved practice.*)

§2. He is empowered to call special meetings of the Grand Lodge—to remove any appointed officer for cause—to fill vacancies occurring among the Grand Officers during the recess of the Grand Lodge—to issue, during the recess, dispensations for opening new Grand and Subordinate Lodges and Encampments, proper application being made—

to issue his dispensation for conferring the three Encampment degrees upon scarlet members petitioning the G. Lodge of the U. States for an Encampment, so as to qualify the petitioners to receive the warrant; provided there be no Encampment in the same State, District, or Territory, in which the applicants can conveniently receive the degrees—to visit officially the Grand and Subordinate Lodges and Encampments, working under the Grand Lodge of the United States, acquaint himself with their proceedings, and to give such instructions and advice as he may deem necessary for the good of the Order.—(*Cons. Arts. XI & XIII; By-Laws, Art. XIII; vol.* 1, *p.* 279, 281, 383, 458; *vol.* 2, *p.* 77–8, *and ancient usage.*)

§3. He is not allowed to vote, except when the Grand Lodge is equally divided. He cannot hold any elective office in any State, District, or Territorial Grand Lodge or Grand Encampment.—(*Cons. Art. IV.*)

§4. All travelling and other expenses, incurred by himself or his deputy, at the opening of a Grand or Subordinate Lodge or Encampment, are to be paid by such Lodge or Encampment.—(*By-Laws, Art. VI.*)

§5. He is authorized to cause two hundred copies of his annual report to be printed before the meeting of the Grand Lodge.—(*Vol.* 1, *p.* 466.)

ARTICLE IV.—DEPUTY GRAND SIRE.

§1. The Deputy Grand Sire is required to open and close all the meetings of the Grand Lodge—to examine the Representatives as to their qualifications, previous to their taking their seats, and make report to the Grand Sire—to support the Grand Sire by his advice and assistance, and in his absence to preside—and in case of the death, disqualification, or refusal to serve of the Grand Sire, to perform the duties of that officer until the next stated meeting.—(*Cons. Arts. V & XIII, By-Laws, Art. XIX.*)

§2. He is authorized, in conjunction with the Grand Sire and Grand Recording Secretary, during the recess of the Grand Lodge, to grant dispensations for opening Grand Lodges or Encampments, or Subordinate Lodges or En-

campments, to be submitted to the Grand Lodge for approval and confirmation at the next annual meeting.—(*By-
Laws, Art. XIII.*)

ARTICLE V.—GRAND RECORDING SECRETARY.

§1. The Grand Recording Secretary is required to make
a just and true record of all the proceedings of the Grand
Lodge—to read all petitions, reports, and communications
addressed to the Grand Lodge—to attest all orders on the
Treasurer, authorized by a vote of the Grand Lodge—to
keep the accounts of the Grand Lodge with the bodies
under its jurisdiction—on application being made for a
Grand Lodge, (or Grand Encampment,) to inform the committee on petitions whether the dues of the Subordinates
are all paid up—to receive the returns of the Grand and
Subordinate Lodges and Encampments under the jurisdiction of the G. Lodge of the U. States—to receive all moneys
for the Grand Lodge, make a record thereof, and forthwith
pay the same over to the Grand Treasurer—to publish a
full statement of the moneys received, specifying the amount,
whence received, and for what paid—to report at each annual communication of the Grand Lodge, in tabular form,
an abstract of the returns of the several Grand and Subordinate Lodges and Encampments—at the same time to
present a statement of all Grand and Subordinate Lodges
and Encampments which may have failed to report—to
furnish the Grand Lodge, in his annual report, with a full
and detailed statement of his receipts and accounts, showing the amounts due to and by it—said report to be made
up to within two weeks of the annual session—to summon
the members to attend at stated and special meetings—to
furnish each Grand Representative, when he takes his seat,
with a copy of the Constitution, Laws and Rules of Order
of the G. Lodge of the United States—to distribute, as soon
as possible, after the close of each communication, copies
of the proceedings among the members of the Grand Lodge
of the United States and the Grand and Subordinate Lodges
and Encampments, after the following rule, to wit, to each
member, one copy; to each Subordinate Lodge and En-

campment, immediately under the jurisdiction of the Grand Lodge of the United States, one copy; and to each Grand Lodge and Grand Encampment, twice as many copies as it has Subordinates under its jurisdiction—and to perform such other duties as the Grand Lodge may from time to time require.—(*Cons. Art. VI,* §1; *By-Laws, Arts.* 3, 11, 19, 21, 22 & 26; *vol.* 1, *p.* 192, 300, 302, 377, 560, *and usage.*)

§2. He has power, in conjunction with the Grand Sire and Deputy Grand Sire, in the recess of the Grand Lodge, to grant dispensations for opening Grand Lodges or Encampments, or Subordinate Lodges or Encampments, to be submitted to the Grand Lodge for approval and confirmation at the next annual meeting.—(*By-Laws, Art. XIII.*)

§3. He is authorized to cause two hundred copies of his annual report to be printed before the meeting of the Grand Lodge.—(*Deduction from Resolution on p.* 466, *vol.* 1.)

§4. He is required to give bond in the sum of two thousand dollars, for the faithful discharge of his duties, to be approved by the Grand Sire.—(*Vol.* 1, *p.* 465.)

§5. He receives for his services such compensation as the Grand Lodge from time to time determines.—(*Cons. Art. VI,* §1.)

ARTICLE VI.—Grand Corresponding Secretary.

§1. The Grand Corresponding Secretary is required to write all letters and communications, and carry on under the direction of the Grand Lodge, or Grand Sire, the correspondence of the Grand Lodge—to make a detailed report, at each annual communication, of the subjects of correspondence, requiring the action of the Grand Lodge—to lay before the Grand Lodge all communications transmitted or received by him—to pay over forthwith, all moneys which he may receive, for the use of the Grand Lodge, to the Grand Recording Secretary, and to transact all such business appertaining to his office as the Grand Lodge may require.—(*Cons. Art. VI,* §2, *vol.* 1, *p.* 288, 302.)

§2. He is authorized to cause 200 copies of his annual

report to be printed before the meeting of the Grand Lodge. —(*Vol.* 1, *p.* 466.)

§3. He receives for his services such compensation as the Grand Lodge from time to time determines.—(*Vol.* 1, *p.* 364, 546, 560 ; *vol.* 2, *p.* 70, 193, 342.)

ARTICLE VII.—GRAND TREASURER.

§1. The Grand Treasurer is required to receive from the Grand Recording Secretary all dues and monies of the Grand Lodge, and give a receipt for the same—pay all orders drawn on him by the Grand Sire attested by the Grand Recording Secretary under the seal of the Grand Lodge; to lay before the Grand Lodge at its annual session, a full and correct statement of his accounts and to furnish in advance a copy thereof to the Grand Recording Secretary to accompany the annual report of said last named officer.—(*Cons. Art. VII, By-Laws, Art. XXII, vol.* 2, *p.* 212-13.)

§2. He shall execute a bond in the sum of $4,000 for the faithful performance of his trust.—(*Vol.* 2, *p.* 216.)

§3. He receives for his services such compensation as the Grand Lodge from time to time determines.—(*Vol.* 1, *p.* 381 ; *vol.* 2, *p.* 214.)

ARTICLE VIII.—APPOINTED OFFICERS.

§1. The Grand Marshal is required when the Grand Lodge of the United States appears in procession, and at Grand Visitations, to take charge thereof, and to make all necessary arrangements for the comfort and accommodation of the officers and members.—(*Usage.*)

§2. The Grand Guardian is required to guard the door of the Grand Lodge room—to prove every brother before he admits him—to prevent the admission of persons not duly qualified—and to permit no one to retire without the P. W.—(*Cons. Art. IX.*)

§3. The Grand Chaplain is required, at the opening and closing of the Grand Lodge, to address the Supreme Ruler of the Universe in prayer.—(*By-Laws, Art. XXVIII.*)

§4. The Grand Messenger is required to prepare the

Grand Lodge room for the meetings of the Grand Lodge—to attend the sessions of the Grand Lodge—to provide the Representatives with such books, papers, or documents as they may require—to deliver, or cause to be delivered, messages from the Grand Officers and Representatives—to take charge of and keep in order the office of the Grand Corresponding Secretary, and to obey the orders of that officer.—(*Vol.* 1, *p.* 560, *and usage.*)

§5. The Grand Messenger receives for his services such compensation as the Grand Lodge from time to time determines.—(*Vol.* 1, *p.* 559; *vol.* 2, *p.* 70, 195, 342.)

ARTICLE IX.—DISTRICT DEPUTY GRAND SIRES.

§1. The Grand Sire is required to appoint, at each annual session of the Grand Lodge, in each State, District, or Territory, (where there are not a Grand Lodge and Grand Encampment) a District Deputy Grand Sire.—(*Vol.* 2, *p.* 189, 215, 305, 338.)

§2. To qualify a brother for the appointment of D. D. Grand Sire, he must be a regular contributing member of a Subordinate Lodge and Encampment, and must have attained the rank of P. G. and the R. P. D.—(*Vol.* 2, *p.* 189, 216.)

§3. District Deputy Grand Sires are required, as the special agents of the Grand Lodge, to do and perform whatever the Grand Lodge or Grand Sire may order to be done in their respective districts—to exercise a general supervision over all Subordinate Lodges and Encampments (in their respective districts) which work under charters granted by the G. L. U. S.—to act as the agents of the Grand Corrresponding Secretary, and obey the special directions of that officer—and to make semi-annual reports of their acts and doings to the Grand Sire.—(*Vol.* 2, *p.* 189, 215–16.)

§4. They are permitted in no case to interfere with the Grand Lodges or Grand Encampments.—(*Vol.* 2, *p.* 189, 216–18.)

§5. Each D. D. G. Sire is required, previous to entering on the duties of his station, to give to the Grand Lodge of the United States a joint and several bond with two sureties, in the sum of $500, conditioned for the faithful discharge of his duties, to be approved by the Grand Sire.—(*Vol.* 2. *p* 213.)

§6. The appintments of D. D. G. Sires may be at any time revoked by the Grand Sire for cause.—(*Vol.* 2, *p.* 189, 216.)

ARTICLE X.—Grand Representatives.

§1. Every Grand Lodge and Grand Encampment, working under a legal, unreclaimed warrant, granted by the Grand Lodge of the United States, is entitled to one vote. Every Grand Lodge and Grand Encampment, having under its jurisdiction more than one thousand contributing members, is entitled to two votes. The number of votes to which each G. Lodge or Grand Encampment may be entitled is to be determined by the annual returns.—(*Cons. Art. X.*)

§2. Representatives must be Past Grands, in good standing, who have received the R. P. degree. They must reside in the State, District or Territory in which the Grand Lodge or Grand Encampment which they claim to represent is located. They must be elected by the Grand Lodge or Grand Encampment which they represent, or appointed by authority thereof, and furnished with a certificate in the following form:

F. L. and T.

To the R. W. Grand Lodge of the United States of the I. O. of O. F.

This certifies that P. G. —— ——, has been duly elected (or appointed) Representative from the Grand Lodge, (or Grand Encampment) of ——, to the Grand Lodge of the United States.

Witness our hands and the Seal of the Grand ——, this —— day of ——.

※※※※
※SEAL※   —— ——, G. Master (or G. Patriarch.)
※※※※   —— ——, G. Secretary, (or G. Scribe.)
                        (*Cons. Art. X, vol.* 2, *p.* 467.)

§3. Representatives must be elected or appointed for the term of two years from the commencement of the annual session of the Grand Lodge of the United States next succeeding their election or appointment.—(*Cons. Art. X, as amended, vol. 2, p. 467.*)

§4. No Representative can represent two Grand bodies at the same time.—(*Cons. Art. X.*)

§5. When a Grand Lodge or Grand Encampment is entitled to two votes and has only one Representative in attendance, such Representative is entitled to the two votes. —(*Vol.* 1, *p.* 301, 525.)

§6. No Grand Lodge or Grand Encampment, in arrears more than one year for dues to the Grand Lodge of the United States, is allowed to vote by its Representative.— (*By-Laws, Art. XII.*)

§7. The Representatives are examined by the Deputy Grand Sire as to their qualifications, previous to being admitted to their seats.　On taking their seats they are furnished with a copy of the Constitution, Laws, and Rules of Order of the Grand Lodge of the United States.—(*By-Laws, Art. XIX.*)

§8. The expenses of each Representative are to be paid by the body which he represents, and should he neglect or refuse to attend the meetings of the Grand Lodge of the United States, when duly notified, he shall be fined five dollars, unless excused by the Grand Lodge.—*By-Laws, Art. XIX.*)

§9. The Representatives, at each session of the Grand Lodge of the United States, are to receive the T. P. W., and they are to deliver the same, on their return, to the Grand Masters of the Grand Lodges, and the Grand Patriarchs of the Grand Encampments.—(*By-Laws, Art. XIV.*)

§10. A Representative has authority, within the jurisdiction which he represents, to introduce a brother without travelling card, or P. W.—(*By-Laws, Art. XVII.*)

§11. The several Grand Lodges and Grand Encampments are required to furnish their Representatives with all documents and papers, necessary in the discharge of the duties of their office.—(*By-Laws, Art. XX.*)

ARTICLE XI.—PAST GRAND SIRES.

§1. The Past Grand Sires are members of the Grand Lodge of the United States for life, and are entitled to vote in all cases. But if they be also Representatives, they cannot vote in both capacities.—(*Cons. Art. VIII.*)

§2. They are not officers of the Grand Lodge.—(*Vol.* 1, *p.* 157.)

ARTICLE XII.—REVENUE.

1. The fee for a Grand or Subordinate warrant, accompanied by the necessary working books, is $30, payable in advance.—(*Cons. Art. XII*, §1 & 2, *By-Laws, Art. VII, and Usage.*)

§2. Subordinate Lodges and Encampments, immediately under the jurisdiction of the Grand Lodge of the United States, are required to pay into its treasury, ten per cent. on their receipts.—(*Cons. Art. XII*, §3.)

§3. Grand Lodges and Grand Encampments, are required to pay $20 per annum for each vote which they are entitled to in the Grand Lodge of the United States.— (*Cons. Art. XII*, §4.)

§4. The last source of revenue is the sale of printed copies of lectures, charges, odes, &c., of the Order, withdrawal and visiting cards and diplomas, the exclusive right to print any and all of which the Grand Lodge of the United States reserves to itself, prohibiting all interference therewith by Grand or Subordinate Lodges or Encampments, or by individuals.—(*Vol.* 1, *p.* 548, *vol.* 2, *p.* 75, 140, 150-1, 211-352.)

§5. The fiscal year of the Grand Lodge commences July 1st, and ends June 30th.—(*Vol.* 2, *p.* 76, 88.)

ARTICLE XIII —MEETINGS.

§1. The regular annual communication is held on the third Monday in September.—(*Cons. Art. XI.*)

§2. The Grand Lodge may meet at any other time on its own adjournment.—(*Cons. Art. XI.*)

§3. Special meetings may be held on the call of the Grand Sire. If the purpose be the granting of a charter, two weeks notice to the Representatives will suffice. But in all other cases two months notice must be given to the different State, District and Territorial Grand Lodges and

Grand Encampments. The purpose of the special meeting must always be communicated with the notice, and no business shall be transacted whereof notice has not been given, as above provided.—(*Cons. Art. XI.*)

§4. The place of meeting may be determined by the Grand Lodge from time to time. The present location is the city of Baltimore, and unless otherwise specially ordered by the Grand Lodge, all meetings are to be held there.—(*Cons. Art. XI, and Journal passim.*)

§5. The hour of meeting is nine A. M.—(*Cons. Art. XI.*)

§6. A majority of Representatives of the several Grand Lodges and G. Encampments is necessary to form a quorum.—(*Cons. Art. XV.*)

§7. Should a quorum not appear at any time appointed for a meeting of the Grand Lodge of the United States, the Grand Sire has power to adjourn the meeting from time to time.—(*Approved practice.*)

§8. The Grand Lodge of the United Sates, works and transacts its business only in the R. P. degree.—(13 *Rule of Order and Usage.*)

§9. Alterations or amendments of the Constitution, or Laws, must be carried by two-thirds of the votes given, but all other questions are to be decided by a majority of votes.—(*Cons. Art. XV, XVI & XVII.*)

§10. Any brother, a member of a Grand Lodge and in possession of the R. P. degree, if recommended by the Representative of the State from which he hails, may be admitted to witness the proceedings of the Grand Lodge of the United States, except when the Grand Lodge is in secret session.—(*Vol. 1, p. 95; vol. 2, p. 123.*)

§11. The Grand Lodge of the United States, may at any time resolve itself into Committee of the whole.—(*Vol. 1, p. 76, 148-9, 151, 447, 449, vol. 2, 123-4, 5, 6.*)

ARTICLE XIV.

AMENDMENTS OF THE CONSTITUTION AND LAWS.

§1. Alterations or amendments of the Constitution of the Grand Lodge of the United States, must be offered in writing at a Stated meeting, and if seconded, they shall be entered on the minutes. At the next stated meeting the amendments may be considered, and if agreed to by two-thirds of the votes given, shall become a part of the Constitution.—(*Cons. Art. XVII.*)

§2. Alterations or amendments of the Laws, must be proposed in writing, at a stated meeting, and may be considered and acted on at the same communication, but not on the same day. Two-thirds of the votes given are necessary to carry such amendments.—(*Cons. Art. XVI, By-Laws, Art. 32.*)

§3. When a proposition to amend the Constitution comes up for action, a motion to amend such proposition cannot be entertained; but a proposition to amend the Laws may be amended.—*Vol. 2, p. 66, 259.*)

§4. A proposition to amend may be indefinitely postponed; or laid on the table.—(*Vol. 2, p. 37-8; vol. 1, p. 446.*)

§5. A proposition to amend may be divided if the sense will admit thereof.—(*Vol. 2, p. 145.*)

§6. A motion to reject a proposition to amend cannot be entertained.—(*Vol. 1, p. 446.*)

§7. An amendment goes into immediate effect on being adopted.—(*Vol. 1, p. 301.*)

§8. But the vote adopting an amendment may be reconsidered at any time during the same communication.—(*Vol. 1, p. 376, 380.*)

DIVISION SECOND.

LAWS OF GENERAL APPLICATION.

~~~~~~~~~~~~~~~~

ARTICLE I.—WARRANTS.

§1. Upon the petition of five brothers in good standing, a warrant to open a Subordinate Lodge in a State, District or Territory, where no Grand Lodge has been established, is granted by the Grand Lodge of the United States, or a dispensation is in like manner granted during recess by the Grand Sire, or by him conjointly with the Deputy Grand Sire and Grand Recording Secretary, subject to the approval of the Grand Lodge at its next annual session.—(*By-Laws Art.* 1, 13. *Vol.* 1, 186, 279, 281.)

§2. The petition must be according to the form in the appendix, and must be accompanied by the fee of thirty dollars, and also by the withdrawal cards of the petitioners, or a certificate from a D. D. G. Sire that the same are in his hands and are in due form.—(*Cons. Art.* 12. *By-Laws, Art.* 7, & *Usage.*)

§3. The Subordinate Lodge is opened by a Past Grand, deputized by the Grand Sire; and it is his duty to deliver to the Lodge the warrant and charge books and to give all necessary instructions.—(*By-Laws, Art.* 1.)

§4. The special deputy makes due return of his proceedings to the Grand Sire.—(*Usage.*)

§5. A warrant or dispensation is in the same manner granted to a Subordinate Encampment in a State, District or Territory, where no Grand Encampment exists, upon the petition of seven members of the Order in good standing, who must have attained to the R. P. Degree. If the brothers proposing to form the Encampment are Scarlet members only, the Grand Sire, upon their petition, instructs a deputy to confer upon them the Encampment degrees, in order to qualify them to petition for a warrant, requiring them to pay the fees for said degrees into the treasury of the new En-

24

campment.—(*By-Laws*, *Art.* 2 *&* 13, *vol.* 1, *p.* 458, *vol.* 2, *p.* 181.)

§6. The petition must be according to the form in the appendix. It must be accompanied by the fee of thirty dollars, and by the withdrawal cards of the petitioners, from the Encampment, of which they were last members, or a certificate from a D. D. G. Sire that the same are in his hands and are in due form.—(*Cons. Art.* 12. *By-Laws, Art.* 2 *& Art.* 7.)

§7. The Subordinate Encampment is opened by the Grand Sire or by a qualified Patriarch by him deputized, who delivers the warrant and charge books, and imparts the necessary instructions.—(*By-Laws, Art. II.*)

§8. The Patriarch specially deputized makes return of his proceedings to the Grand Sire.—(*Usage.*)

§9. A warrant or dispensation is in the same manner granted by the Grand Lodge of the United States, upon the petition of three or more Subordinate Lodges in a State, District or Territory where no Grand Lodge has been established, to open a Grand Lodge.—(*By-Laws, Art. IV.*)

§10. The Lodges petitioning must contain seven Past Grands in good standing.—(*By-Laws, Art. IV.*)

§11. The petition must be according to the form in the appendix, and is prepared and authenticated in the following manner. Each Lodge in the proposed jurisdiction appoints one or more of its Past Grands to represent it in a convention, notified to meet at a convenient time and place, and to be composed of the Representatives of the several Lodges, and furnishes such Representatives with a statement under its seal of the number of its Past Grands in good standing. The questions of the propriety of application, and location of the Grand Lodge, are determined by a majority, comprising at least three Lodges, the vote being by Lodges. The non-attendance of a Lodge by its representative does not vitiate the proceedings if the Lodges present be sufficient in number to fulfil the foregoing requirements. The petition must be accompanied by the fee of thirty dollars. —(*By-Laws, Art. V & VII, vol.* 2, *p.* 345, 363.)

§12. The Grand Lodge is opened by the Grand Sire, or

by a qualified brother by him specially deputized, who conveys the warrant, imparts all necessary instructions, and makes return to the Grand Sire.—(*By-Laws, Art. IV.*)

§13. A warrant or dispensation is in like manner granted to open a Grand Encampment in a State, District or Territory where no Grand Encampment has been established, upon the petition of three or more Subordinate Encampments which contain seven Past Chief Patriarchs in good standing, the petition being accompanied by the fee of thirty dollars.—(*By-Laws, Arts. IV & VII.*)

§14. The petition must be according to the form in the appendix, and must be prepared and authenticated in the same manner as provided for the authentication of petitions for G. Lodges, save that the convention is composed of Patriarchs as representatives of the Subordinate Encampments, and each Encampment furnishes its Representative or Representatives with a statement, under seal, of its number of P. C. Patriarchs in good standing.—(*By-Laws, Art. V, vol. 2, p. 345, 363.*)

§15. The Grand Encampment is opened by the Grand Sire, or by some qualified brother by him specially deputized, who conveys the warrant, imparts the necessary instructions, and makes due return to the Grand Sire.—*By-Laws, Art. IV.*)

§16. The expenses of the officer attending to open a Lodge or Encampment, Grand or Subordinate, are paid by such Lodge or Encampment.—(*By-Laws, Art. VI.*)

§17. If a petition for a warrant be in any case denied, the fee is repaid to the petitioners.—(*By-Laws, Art. VII.*)

§18. The Grand Lodge of the United States will not grant a warrant or confirm a dispensation, to open a Grand Lodge or Grand Encampment, unless the Subordinates petitioning have paid up their dues, and information in this respect is communicated to the Committee on Petitions by the Grand Recording Secretary, before the petition is considered.—(*Vol. 1, p. 192, 560.*)

§19. The warrant of a Grand Lodge or Grand Encampment having been granted, all Subordinate Lodges or Encampments, within its territorial limits, immediately pass under the jurisdiction of said Grand Lodge or Encampment. But when a Grand Lodge or Grand Encampment is opened by dispensation during recess, its Subordinates are required to pay their dues to the Grand Lodge of the United States, until the confirmation of the dispensation.—(*By-Laws, Art. XVI, vol.* 1, *p.* 560.)

§20. Upon the establishment of a Grand Lodge or Grand Encampment, the application for the renewal of the warrant of a Subordinate Lodge or Encampment which had previously become extinct, must be made to the Grand Lodge of the United States with the sanction of the Grand Lodge or Grand Encampment of the State, District or Territory.—(*Vol* 2, *p.* 195.)

§21. Every Lodge or Encampment, Grand or Subordinate, receiving a warrant from the Grand Lodge of the United States, continues to exist so long as it consists of five members in good standing, if a Lodge, and seven if an Encampment; except its warrant be reclaimed by special act, and such warrant cannot be restored, nor can the name and number of any Lodge or Encampment, be assigned to any persons, save to a sufficient number of those who were members of said Lodge or Encampment before the extinction of its warrant. And this law is imperative upon all Grand Lodges and Encampments, in regard to their Subordinates.—(*Vol.* 1, *p.* 53, 75-6, 370.)

§22. Upon the forfeiture or annulment of a warrant, a Lodge or Encampment, Grand or Subordinate, under the jurisdiction of the Grand Lodge of the United States, is required to surrender to the G. Recording Secretary its warrant, books, documents, funds and property, to be returned upon its renewal, as before provided.—(*Vol.* 2, *p.* 350, *and approved practice.*)

ARTICLE II.—REGALIA.

Regalia for Subordinate Lodges.

§1. The regalia of a member who has taken only the Initiatory degree is a plain white apron, without collar or any other badge of distinction.—(*Vol.* 1, *p.* 541.)

§2. The aprons and collars of members of Subordinate Lodges are *White.*

Those for members of the *First* deg. are trimmed with *White.*

"	"	"	Second	"	"	*Pink.*
"	"	"	*Third*	"	"	*Blue.*
"	"	".	*Fourth*	"	"	*Green.*
"	"	"	*Fifth*	"	"	*Scarlet.*

The N. G. wears a *Scarlet* collar, trim'd with white or silver.

"	V. G.	"	*Blue*	"	"	"	"	"
"	Secretaries	*Green*	"	"	"	"	"
"	Treasurer	*Green*	"	"	"	"	"

The Supporters of the N. G. wear Scarlet sashes.

" " " V. G. wear Blue sashes.

The Warden and Conductor wear Black sashes.

The Scene Supporters wear White sashes.

The Chaplain wears a White sash.

The aprons of the elective and appointed officers are White, trimmed with the color of the collar or sash indicated for the office.—(*By-Laws, Art. XXV.*)

§3. Past Grands wear *Scarlet* collars or sashes—and aprons, either *White* trimmed with *Scarlet* or *Scarlet* trimmed with *White.* The aprons and collars of Past Grands may be trimmed with silver lace or fringe. Those who have taken the R. P. degree may have trimmings of *Yellow* metal.—(*By-Laws, Art. XXV.*)

§4. All members of a Subordinate Lodge may wear *Rosettes,* displaying the colors of the degrees they have taken.—(*By-Laws, Art. XXV.*)

Jewels for Officers of Subordinate Lodges.

§5.—The jewel for P. G. is five pointed *Star.*

"	"	N. G. is *Crossed Gavils*
"	"	V. G. is *Hour Glass.*
"	"	Secretary is *Crossed Pens.*
"	"	Treasurer is *Crossed Keys.*
"	"	Warden is *Crossed Wands.*
"	"	Conductor is *Crossed Axes.*
"	"	Guardian is *Crossed Swords.*

—*Ancient Usage.*)

Jewels for Officers of Grand Lodge.

§6.—The jewel for P. G. M. is the *Sun* with *Hand and Heart.*

The jewel for Grand Master is *Sun,* with the scales of justice impressed or engraved thereon.

The jewel for D. G. M. is *Half Moon.*

"   Warden is *Crossed Gavels.*
"   Grand Secretary is *Crossed Pens.*
"   Grand Treasurer is *Crossed Keys.*
"   Grand Conductor is *Roman Sword.*
"   Grand Guardian is *Crossed Swords.*
"   Grand Marshal is *Baton.*

—(*Ancient Usage.*)

§7. All of said jewels shall be of White metal.

Regalia for Grand Lodges.

§8. The Officers and Past Grands of a Grand Lodge, wear the regalia of a Past Grand, as before defined.—(*By-Laws, Art. XXV.*)

Regalia for Officers of Grand and Subordinate Encampments.

§9. The *Regalia* for an officer of a Grand Encampment, is a royal purple *Collar* or *Sash,* and *Black Apron* trimmed with gold bullion fringe.

§10. The *Regalia* for an officer of a Subordinate Encampment is a *Purple Collar,* and *Black Apron* trimmed with gold colored fringe or lace, or both.

Jewels for Officers of Grand and Subordinate Encampments.

§11. For *Grand Patriarch,* a double triangle of Yellow metal, with a representation of an Altar and Crossed Crooks in the centre.

For *Grand High Priest,* same triangle with representation of the Breast-plate.

For Grand S. W., same triangle, with Crossed Crooks.
"   J. W.,   "   Single Crook.
"   Scribe,   "   Crossed Pens.
"   Treasurer,   "   Crossed Keys.
"   Sentinel,   "   Crossed Swords.

§12. For officers of Subordinate Encampments *Single*

3*

Triangle, otherwise as designated for officers of Grand Encampments.

§13. All Past Officers of Grand and Subordinate Encampments are entitled to wear the regalia and jewels appertaining to the offices they have passed.—(*Vol.* 2, *p.* 339, 362.)

Regalia for members of Grand and Subordinate Encampments.

§14. Members of Grand or Subordinate Encampments, shall wear Purple Collars, Black Aprons and Black Gloves. The Aprons and Collars trimmed with Yellow lace or fringe. —(*By-Laws, Art. XXV.*)

Funeral Regalia.

§15. The regalia to be worn by all brothers attending the funeral of a deceased brother is as follows :—A black crape rosette, having a centre of the color of the highest degree to which the wearer may have attained, to be worn on the left breast; above it a sprig of evergreen, and below it (if the wearer be an officer or past officer,) the jewel or jewels, which as such he may be entitled to wear.(—*Vol.* 2, *p.* 357-8.)

§16. The ordinary mourning badge to be worn by brothers, in memory of a deceased brother, is a strip of black crape passed through one button-hole of the left lapel of the coat, and tied with a narrow ribbon of the color of the highest degree to which the wearer has attained.—(*Vol.* 2, *p.* 357-8.)

Visiters.

§17. Past Officers, and members in possession of Encampment degrees, and all other members of the Order, when *visiting* Grand or Subordinate Lodges, are entitled to wear the regalia and jewels pertaining to the highest degree which they have taken.—(*By-Laws, Art. XXXI.*)

G. L. U. S.

§18. The Grand Representatives in the G. L. U. S. appear in the proper regalia of the bodies which they respectively represent.—(*Vol.* 1, *p.* 378, *By-Law,* 25 ; *vol.* 2, *p.* 508-19.)

ARTICLE III.—Public Occasions.

§1. All processions and balls at which the regalia, emblems, &c., of the Order are to be used, are prohibited, unless permission therefor be granted, after due consideration, in open Grand Lodge, or by the Grand Master in the recess of the Grand Lodge.—(*Vol.* 1, *p.* 352-3.)

§2. All publications made in any newspaper, calling on the Order to appear in regalia, on any occasion not authorized by the proper Grand Lodge are incorrect, and obnoxious to censure; and the unauthorized use of the name of the Order is strictly forbidden.—(*Vol.* 1, *p.* 352-3.)

§3. The delivery of Lectures on Odd-Fellowship, either in Lodges, or in public, is not consistent with the duties of brethren of the Order, unless they are authorized to act in such a capacity by special enactment in Lodges of the State, District or Territory, within whose jurisdiction the lectures are delivered; and all enactments of Grand or Subordinate Lodges, having such an object in view, should expire by limitation within some reasonable space of time.—(*Vol.* 2, *p.* 57.)

§4. In all processions of the Order the rules of precedence set forth in the succeeding article, so far as they may admit of being followed, are to be adhered to.—(*Vol.* 2, *p.* 358.)

ARTICLE IV.—Funeral Ceremonies.

§1. The order of procedure at the funeral of a deceased brother is as follows:

At the appointed hour the Subordinate Lodge of which such a brother was a member, shall meet at its Lodge room. The N. G. shall appoint a Marshal and such number of Assistant Marshals as may be required. The Lodge shall thereupon move, and the brothers shall pass in procession from the Lodge room to the place from which the funeral may be appointed to start, in the following order:

1. The Marshal, wearing a black scarf, and bearing a baton bound with a band of black crape.

2. The O. G. bearing a red staff in like mourning.

3. The Scene Supporters bearing white wands in like mourning.

4. Members of the Initiatory Degree, two abreast.

5. Members of the White, Pink, Royal Blue, Green and Scarlet Degrees, respectively, in like order.

6. Members of the Lodge having the Patriarchal, G. R. and R. P. Degrees, respectively, in like order.

7. The I. G., bearing the regalia and insignia indicative of the rank in the Order of the deceased brother.

8. The Treasurer and Secretaries of the Lodge.

9. The V. G., supported by his R. and L. Supporters, each bearing his wand of office, bound with a band of black crape.

10. The Chaplain, wearing a white scarf, and supported by the Warden and Conductor, each bearing his staff of office in like mourning.

11. The N. G., supported by his R. and L. Supporters, each bearing his wand of office in like mourning.

12. The Past Grands of the Lodge, two abreast.

13. Brethren of invited Lodges, those of each Lodge arranged in the order above prescribed; the Lodges, when more than one may be represented, arranged in order of juniority.

§2. On arriving at the place appointed for the starting of the funeral, the brothers shall take position in the above order, immediately before the corpse, and shall precede it to the place of interment.

§3. On arriving at the place of interment, the procession shall open to the right and left, and allow the corpse, mourners, &c., to pass through, the brothers on either side uncovered, the hat held in the left hand of each, and joining hands with each other. And after the passing of the corpse, mourners, &c., between the two lines, the brothers shall again form in reversed order and proceed to the grave.

§4. After the performance of such religious service as the friends of the deceased may cause to be there performed, and before the final closing of the grave, the brothers shall form silently, and as nearly as may be according to the order above set forth, uncovered, the hat in the left hand of each, and joining hands with each other, in one or more circles, as regular as the nature of the ground may admit, around the grave ; when the Chaplain, or in default of a Chaplain, the N. G. may address the brothers and offer up a prayer, or may address the brothers without the offering of a prayer ; and after such address or prayer, or both, or if there be no address or prayer, then after a pause suited to the solemnity of the occasion, the N. G. shall advance singly to the head of the grave, and cast into it with the right hand the sprig of evergreen from his regalia, and shall return to his place ; whereupon the brothers from left to right in regular succession, and in such numbers at a time as not to cause confusion, shall advance to the grave shall cast into it (each with the right hand) the sprig of evergreen from their regalia, and shall return to their place. And after all have done this, and the grave shall have been filled up or closed, the brothers shall silently form again in procession according to the order observed in coming to the place of interment, and shall return in such order to the Lodge room, where the N. G. shall declare the funeral ceremonies to be closed.

§5. If at the time of his death the deceased brother was a member of an Encampment, or of a State, District, or Territorial Grand Lodge or Grand Encampment, or of the Grand Lodge of the United States, the Chaplain and highest Officer or Officers present, of such Encampment, or Grand body or bodies, supported each by two members thereof, shall take position in the funeral procession next after the Chaplain and N. G. respectively, of the Subordinate Lodge of the deceased, and shall take precedence of such N. G. and of each other according to their respective rank in conducting the ceremony of interment as above set forth.—(*Vol.* 2, *p.* 357-8.)

ARTICLE V.— DIPLOMAS.

§1. The Grand Lodge of the United States has prescribed a form of certificate or diploma (in English, French and German,) to be issued to members of the Order in good standing.—(*Vol.* 1, *p.* 246, 287, *and see form in appendix.*)

§2. If any Grand Lodge or Grand Encampment declines the agency for the sale of Diplomas, then the G. R. Secretary of the Grand Lodge of the United States is authorized to appoint the Grand Secretary or Grand Scribe of such Grand Lodge or Grand Encampment, and in the event of their declining, any other person, satisfactory security being given.—(*Vol.* 2, *p.* 200, 523.)

§3. The Grand Recording Secretary is authorized to furnish the diplomas to Subordinate Lodges and Encampments, where Grand Lodges do not exist.—(*Vol.* 1, *p.* 287, 317.)

§4. The diplomas are signed by the Grand Recording Secretary of the Grand Lodge of the United States, and when issued to members of the Order by State Grand Lodges and Grand Encampments, or by Subordinate Lodges and Encampments, immediately under the jurisdiction of the Grand Lodge of the United States, are authenticated by the signatures of the presiding Officer and Recording Secretary or Scribe of the Body by which they are issued.— (*Vol.* 1, *p.* 287; *vol.* 2, *p.* 196.)

§5. Every member of the Grand Lodge is presented with a blank diploma, signed by the Grand Sire and Grand Recording Secretary, which is to be filled up after a form specially prescribed.—(*Vol.* 1, *p.* 287, 310, 311, *and see form in application.*)

§6. The Grand Recording Secretary has discretionary power during the recess of the Grand Lodge to cause to be printed from time to time, such number of copies of the diploma as may be necessary.—(*Vol.* 2, *p.* 53.)

ARTICLE VI.—The T. P. W.

§1. The T. P. W. was adopted for the protection of the Order, and is one of the tests by which travelling brothers are tried.—(*Vol.* 1, *p.* 24; *vol.* 2, *p.* 60, 66.)

§2. It is designed only for the use of brethren who are travelling beyond the limits of the jurisdiction to which they belong, and in order that each brother entitled to it may be properly instructed therein, and that visiting brethren from other jurisdictions may be properly examined, the N. G. and V. G. of a Lodge, and the C. P. and S. W. of an Encampment are to be privately put in possession thereof at the time of their installation, that they may be qualified either to give or receive it. The Grand Master and Grand Patriarch of a State and their regular deputies, should, of course, also, be in possession of it.—(*Vol.* 2, *p.* 60, 66, 360, 338.)

§3. None other than members who are placed in some of the positions above mentioned are entitled to receive it.— (*Vol.* 2, *p.* 60, 66.)

§4. It is selected by the Grand Sire, is changed annually, and goes into use on the first day of January in each year. —(*By-Laws*, *Art. XIV*, vol. 1, *p.* 381.)

§5. It is the duty of the Grand Sire to communicate it to the Grand Representatives at each annual session, and it is their duty to deliver it in their several States, to the Grand Master and Grand Patriarch.—(*By-Laws*, *Art. XIV.*)

§6. If any State be without a Grand Representative, it is the duty of the Grand Sire to transmit the word, in due season, through some other safe channel, to the State authorities, (if there be any,) or to the N. G. of each Lodge and the C. P. of each Encampment working under the jurisdiction of the Grand Lodge of the United States.—(*By-Laws*, *Art. XIV.*)

§7. By the terms of the independent Charter, granted to the Grand Lodge of British North America, the T. P. W. is the same in both jurisdictions and is to be selected (as above provided) by the United States authorities. It is the duty of the Grand Sire of the United States to communicate the word to the Grand Sire of British North America. (*Vol.* 2, *p.* 328–9.)

§8. As a general rule the T. P. W. can only be given by a N. G. or C. P. to the members of their own bodies respectively; but when brothers are called from home suddenly, without time to make personal application for their visiting cards, it is proper to accompany the card, when forwarded, by a letter from the N. G. of the Lodge granting it, to the N. G. of some Lodge in the place where the travelling brother is temporarily resident, which letter conveys a request that the P. W. should be communicated.—(*Vol.* 2, *p.* 454.)

ARTICLE VII.—CARDS.

§1. The Grand Lodge of the United States has prescribed the forms of visiting and withdrawal cards to be exclusively used throughout its jurisdiction.—(*Vol.* 2, *p.* 73–5, *and see appendix.*)

§2. Any brother in good standing may, by application, (personal or otherwise,) to his Lodge or Encampment, obtain a *visiting* card to be valid for any reasonable length of time expressed on its face.—(*Vol.* 2, *p.* 73–5.)

§3. Any brother in good standing, may in the same mode obtain a withdrawal card.—(*Vol.* 2, *p.* 74–5.)

§4. Brethren holding visiting cards continue to be members of the Order and are amenable to all the laws of their Lodges or Encampments, in the same manner as other members.—(*Vol.* 2, *p.* 74.)

§5. Visiting cards entitle brothers holding them, to visit Lodges or Encampments, as the case may be, while travelling or sojourning in places beyond the limits of the jurisdiction to which they belong. They also entitle the holders to all the courtesies of the brotherhood, as well as the benevolent usage of the Order, if they should meet with accident or misfortune.—(*Vol.* 2, *p.* 73–5.)

§6. The vote of a Subordinate Lodge or Encampment, granting a withdrawal card to a brother applying therefor, severs the connection of such brother with such Lodge or Encampment, and releases the Lodge or Encampment granting it from all liabilities for benefits, whether the card is actually taken or not. But if the card be taken, the brother receiving it is entitled to the T. P. W. in use at the time and retains the right to visit with that word for a year.—(*Vol.* 2, *p.* 73, 312.)

§7. Every visiting or withdrawal card must bear the counter-signature of the Grand Corresponding Secretary of the Grand Lodge of the United States or a fac-simile thereof. It must be signed by the N. G. or C. P. and attested by the Secretary or Scribe, under the seal of the Lodge or Encampment granting it. The name of the holder must also be written on the margin in his own hand-writing.—(*By-Laws, Art. XVII*; vol. 1, *p.* 302, vol. 2, *p.* 212, 307 *and Usage.*)

§8. When the time has expired for which a visiting card was granted, it is the duty of the brother holding it to return it to the Lodge or Encampment which granted it.—*(An-cient Usage.)*

§9. A member may by written resignation withdraw from the Order and is not bound to take a withdrawal card.—*(Vol. 2, p. 201.)*

§10. The Lodge or Encampment granting a visiting or withdrawal card has power to recall or annul the same for good cause.—*(Ancient Usage.)*

§11. No Lodge or Encampment is *bound* to receive a card on deposit (that is to admit the holder to membership) but such cases are to be governed by the rules prescribed by the local authorities.—*(Vol. 2, p. 75-6.)*

§12. The Grand Lodge of the United States has adopted a form of card or certificate for the wives and widows of Odd-Fellows.—*(Vol. 2, p. 210, and see appendix.)*

§13. Each Subordinate Lodge may by a vote of two-thirds of its members present, grant a card to the wife or widow of any member on application therefor, to be signed by the officers of the Lodge and countersigned by the recipient on the margin.—*(Vol. 2, p. 210.)*

§14. Such card, if granted to the wife of a member, cannot remain in force more than one year, but if granted to a widow it continues valid during her widowhood.—*(Vol. 2, p. 210.)*

§15. The Grand Recording Secretary is required to furnish certificates, in the nature of withdrawal cards, to all members of Subordinate Lodges or Encampments, (immediately under the jurisdiction of the G. L. U. S.) which may become extinct.—*(Vol. 2, p. 455.)*

§16. Such certificates are signed by the Grand Recording Secretary and attested by the seal of the G. L. U. S. They entitle the holder to all the privileges exercised under withdrawal cards, and are only to be issued after the presentation by the applicants of satisfactory evidence of membership and good standing.—*(Vol. 2, p. 455.)*

ARTICLE VIII.—Travelling Brothers.

§1. When a visiting brother presents himself at the door of a Lodge or Encampment, it is his duty to send in his card

4

by the Guardian or Sentinel. If the card be authentic, the presiding officer appoints a committee of three to examine the visiter. In a Lodge, one member of this committee must be the N. G. himself, the V. G. or some other brother known to be in possession of the T. P. W. and the other members must be of the Scarlet Degree. In an Encampment, one member must be the C. P. himself, the S. W. or some Patriarch known to be in possession of the T P. W., and the other members must of course be of the R. P. Degree.—(*Vol.* 2, *p.* 86.)

§2. It is the duty of the proper member of the examining committee in the first place to obtain the T. P. W. privately from the visiter; the word is to be lettered and the visiter must commence. The committee must then examine the visiter in the degree in which the Lodge or Encampment is open, and *in cases of doubt*, they may extend their examination to the other degrees.—(*Vol.* 2, *p.* 86.)

§3. If the examining committee be satisfied with the result of the examination, they will introduce the visiter into the Lodge or Encampment without further ceremony.--(*Vol.* 2, *p.* 308, 510.)

§4. No brother can be admitted to visit or deposite his card in a Lodge or Encampment, out of the State, District, or Territory where he resides, unless he presents a regular card authenticated in the manner pointed out by section 7 of the Article next preceding this, and prove himself in the mode pointed out in this Article; provided, nevertheless, a brother may always visit, if introduced by a Grand Representative or other elective Grand Officer of the jurisdiction under which he wishes to visit.—(*By-Laws, Art. XVII.*)

§5. When a brother applies for and obtains relief from a Lodge or Encampment of which he is not a member, the amount of relief granted must be endorsed upon his card, and notice thereof must be forwarded to the Lodge or Encampment granting the card, by the Secretary or Scribe of the Lodge or Encampment granting the relief.—(*Vol.* 2, *p.* 299.)

§6. A test O. B. N. is no part of the mode of examining visiters, and any Lodge or Encampment introducing any such requirement, would deserve severe censure.—(*Vol.* 2, *p.* 470.)

ARTICLE IX.—RETURNS.

§1. Every Grand Lodge is required to make an annual return to the Grand Lodge of the United States, according to the forms in the appendix; the same to be furnished by the G. L. U. S.—(*By-Laws, Art.* 11;--*Vol.* 2, *p.* 88.)

§2. The return is in two parts. The first part contains full information under the following heads:

1. Names and numbers of Subordinate Lodges.
2. Place and times of their meeting.
3. Number of initiations.
4. Number of rejections.
5. Number admitted by card.
6. "   withdrawn by card.
7. "   re-instatements.
8. "   suspensions.
9. "   expulsions.
10. "   deaths.
11. "   Past Grands.
12. "   contributing members.
13. Whole amount of receipts.
14. Names of the Grand Masters.
15. Names of Past Grand Officers.
16. Number of its members.
17. Names of persons expelled and suspended for cause other than non-payment of dues, are required to be appended to this return.—(*By-Laws, Art.* 11—*Vol.* 1, *p.* 304, 568.)

§3. The second part contains full information under the following heads:

1. Number of brothers relieved in Subordinate Lodges.
2. "   widowed families.
3. "   brothers buried.
4. Amount paid for relief of brothers.
5. "   relief of widowed families.
6. "   education of orphans.
7. "   burying the dead.

8. Total amount paid for these purposes.

9. Such supplementary information as may be useful to the Order, and explanatory of the foregoing.—(*By-Laws, Art.* 11—*Vol.* 1, *p.* 572.)

§4. The return, attested in both of its parts by the signatures of the Grand Master and the Grand Secretary, and the seal of the Grand Lodge, must be rendered to the G. Recording Secretary, at least one month previous to the annual session of the Grand Lodge of the United States.—(*By-Laws, Art.* 11.)

§5. The return must correspond to the fiscal year of the Grand Lodge of the United States, commencing on the first day of July, and terminating on the thirtieth of June.—(*Vol.* 2, *p.* 76, 88.)

§6. Every Grand Encampment is required to make returns similar to those required of Grand Lodges, and according to the form in appendix. They must contain the number of Past Chief Patriarchs and Past High Priests, and the names of Past Grand Patriarchs, and must be attested by the Grand Patriarch and Grand Scribe, under the seal of the Grand Encampment. They must be rendered to the G. Recording Secretary, at least one month previous to the session of the Grand Lodge of the United States.—(*By-Laws, Art.* 11.)

§7. Each Subordinate Lodge under the jurisdiction of the Grand Lodge of the United States, is required to make returns semi-annually, according to the forms in the appendix. The returns set forth:

1. Names of persons initiated.
2.   "   brothers admitted by card.
3.   "   persons rejected.
4.   "   brothers withdrawn by card.
5.   "   "   suspended, and the cause in each case specified.
6. Names of brothers expelled, and the cause in each case specified.
7. Names of brothers re-instated.
8.   "   "   deceased during the term.
9. Number of degrees conferred.

10. Number of contributing members.

11. Whole amount of receipts, specifying the amount from each source of revenue.

12. Amount of dues to the G. L. U. S., being ten per centum on the whole amount of receipts.

13. Names of officers elected and installed.—(*By-Laws, Art. 3 and 11.*)

§8. Each Subordinate Lodge under the jurisdiction of the Grand Lodge of the United States, must also make a relief return, according to the form in the appendix, and embracing the same details, so far as they are applicable, as are required in the returns from Grand Lodges.—(*By-Laws, Art. 3 and 11.*)

§9. These returns must be attested by the N. G., V. G. and Secretary of the Subordinate Lodge under its seal; and accompanied by its dues, must be rendered to the D. G. S. of the District in which it is situated, immediately after the close of each term.—(*By-Laws, Art. 3; vol. 1, p. 569.*)

§10. Each Subordinate Encampment under the jurisdiction of the Grand Lodge of the United States, must in like manner make semi-annual returns to that body, according to form in the appendix—such returns to correspond in all respects with the returns from Subordinate Lodges, and to be attested by the G. P., H. P. and Scribe, under seal of the Encampment. They must be rendered, accompanied by the dues, to the Deputy Grand Sire of the District in which the Encampment is situated, immediately after the close of each term.—(*By-Laws, Art. 11.*)

§11. Any Subordinate Lodge or Encampment under the jurisdiction of the Grand Lodge of the United States, which fails for one year to make its returns, forfeits its charter.—(*Vol. 2, p. 76, 88.*)

ARTICLE X.—LOCAL LAWS.

§1. The Constitution of all Grand and Subordinate Lodges and Encampments, (under the immediate jurisdiction of the Grand Lodge of the United States,) and all amendments thereto, are to be forwarded to the G. L. U. S. on their adoption, for examination. If approved, they become the organic law. If error be found the error must be corrected. In the interval between the adoption of the constitution, or amendment, and its confirmation by the G. L. U. S., it is binding on the body by which it has been adopted.—(*By-Laws, Art.* 10; *Vol.* 2, *p.* 454.)

§2. The G. L. U. S. has abundant power to direct any Grand Lodge or Grand Encampment to remove any clause or article from its Constitution or By-Laws, which may conflict with the fundamental laws of the Order, even though said Constitution or By-Laws may have been approved.— *(Journal, Vol.* 2, *p.* 486.)

§3. The G. L. U. S. has no power to alter the charter of a State Grand Lodge or Grand Encampment, without the consent of such Grand Lodge or Grand Encampment. *(Journal, Vol.* 2, *p.* 486.)

DIVISION THIRD.

GRAND AND SUBORDINATE LODGES.

ARTICLE I.—GRAND LODGES.

Origin, Organization, Relations to the G. L. U. S.

§1. Grand Lodges exist by virtue of warrants or dispensations, granted or confirmed by the Grand Lodge of the United States; and they have jurisdiction over all the Subordinate Lodges within their assigned limits.—(*Cons., Art. 1.—By-Laws, Art. IV, XVI.*

§2. Grand Lodges are not allowed to change their location, without the consent of the Grand Lodge of the United States. Nor can more than one Grand Lodge exist in one State, District or Territory at the same time.—(*By-Laws, Art. VIII.—Vol, 1. p. 272-3, 379 vol. 2, p. 55.*

§3. The Grand Lodges work in the G. L. Degree.— (*Usage.*)

§4. The quorum of a Grand Lodge consists of five or more members. If there be less than five members, it becomes disqualified to work—its warrant is at once forfeited, and its Subordinates pass under the jurisdiction of the Grand Lodge of the United States.—(*Vol. 1, 75-76, Hopkins D., 1 series, No. 58.*)

§5. Each Grand Lodge consists of all the Past Grands in good standing within its jurisdiction; but by its Constitution it may restrict its legislative power to such representative basis, as it may deem best for the proper transaction of business; but it cannot abridge the privileges of Past Grands pertaining to their rank in the degrees of the Order; viz: their right to past official degrees, eligibility to office, precedence belonging to their grade, privilege of attending the meetings of their Grand Lodge, and right to vote for Grand officers.—(*Hopkins D., 1 series, No. 49, No. 58.— Ibid, 2d series, No. 61, approved practice, Vol. 2, p. 480.*)

§6. A Past Grand cannot be a member of more than one Grand Lodge at the same time. A Past Grand from one State does not of right become a member of a Grand Lodge in another State, upon becoming a resident within its jurisdiction.—(*By-Laws, Art. XV., Hopkins D.*, 1 *series, No.* 58.)

§7. Each State Grand Lodge must confer the G. L. degree, without pecuniary consideration, upon any brother in good standing, who has regularly performed the duties of Noble Grand in a Subordinate Lodge, and upon no other person; it being a reward for meritorious service; and it must confer the Past official degrees upon all Past Grands entitled thereto.—(*By-Laws, Art. XXIX.—Vol.* 2, *p.* 191.)

§8. Each Grand Lodge has a Grand Seal, an impression of which in wax must be deposited in the office of the Grand Recording Secretary of the G. L. U. S. It must adopt a Constitution, subject to the approval of the Grand Lodge of the United States; and one month at least prior to the annual session, it must make to that body annual returns of the condition of the Order within its jurisdiction, according to the forms in the appendix, accompanied with its dues. It may not change its Constitution in such manner as to abridge the terms of its officers then incumbent, and it is responsible to the Grand Lodge of the United States for any irregularity in work, or otherwise, which it may allow within its jurisdiction.—(*By-Laws, Articles* 9, 10, 11, 23. —*Vol* 2, *p.* 346.—*Hopkins D.*, 2 *series, No.* 117.)

§9. Each Grand Lodge is entitled to one representative in the Grand Lodge of the United States; and if the Subordinates within its jurisdiction contain one thousand members, the fact appearing in the annual return, it is entitled to two representatives. It must pay the expenses of its representatives, and furnish them with certificates in proper form, and with all documents and papers necessary for the performance of their duties. It must pay to the Grand Lodge of the United States twenty dollars for every vote to which it is entitled therein; and its representatives shall not be allowed to vote, if it be more than one year in arrears. It may nominate by its representatives a candidate for the office of Grand Sire, and a candidate for the office of D. G. Sire.—(*Constitution, Articles* 10, 12.—*By-Laws, Articles* 12, 20. *Cons. Art.* 14.)

§10. Every Grand Lodge must enforce upon her Subordinates a strict adherence to the work of the Order, according to the forms determined upon by the Grand Lodge of the United States ; and it cannot use, nor suffer to be used within its jurisdiction, any charges, lectures, degrees, forms of installation, ceremonies, or regalia, other than those prescribed by the Grand Lodge of the United States. It must enact laws to prevent its Subordinates from initiating persons who reside under the jurisdiction of other Grand Lodges, as well as from initiating persons at places remote from their permanent residence, while Lodges are situated in their immediate neighborhood.—(*By-Laws, Art.* 23, 30.)

§11. Grand Lodges are required to enact laws to restrict processions and public displays in regalia, within their respective jurisdictions ; and to regulate the delivery of lectures upon matters connected with the Order.—*Vol.* 1, *p.* 352, *Vol.* 2; *p.* 57, 200.)

§12. Each Grand Lodge is entitled to receive as many printed copies of the annual proceedings of the Grand Lodge of the United States, as it has in number Subordinates working under its jurisdiction, for its own use ; and an equal number to be distributed among its Subordinates.—(*By-Laws, Art.* 21.)

ARTICLE II.—GRAND LODGES.

Powers, Duties, Relations to Subordinates.

§1. Each Grand Lodge is the grand legislative head of the Order in its jurisdiction.—(*Vol.* 1, *p.* 456, 538.)

§2. A Grand Lodge has power to grant charters to Subordinate Lodges, and to open such Lodges according to the prescribed form. It may enact laws for the government of its Subordinates. It may establish the form of returns from Subordinates, and fix upon the periods when they shall be made ; and it may impose such dues upon its Subordinates as shall be necessary to defray its expenses —(*General Principle and Usage.*)

§3. Each Grand Lodge has power upon appeal to hear and determine upon matters of grievance between members, and Lodges within its jurisdiction. No Lodge can appeal from its decision to the Grand Lodge of the United States but with its consent, save in case of an expelled Lodge, which surrenders its effects. It may grant a new trial to a member of a Subordinate Lodge, on the ground of informality or unfairness, or discovery of new testimony. It has power of interference and adjustment, in difficulties arising between one of its Subordinates and a Subordinate in another jurisdiction.—(*Cons. Art.* 1, *vol.* 2, *p.* 51, 213, —*vol.* 1, *p.* 238)

§4. Each Grand Lodge is possessed of full executive powers over its Subordinates. It enforces their obedience to the laws of the Grand Lodge of the United States, as well as to its own. It may suspend or annul the charter of a Lodge for sufficient cause, but cannot restore the same to any but its original holders. It cannot compel a Subordinate Lodge to meet in a particular room, but may prohibit it from meeting in a room obviously unsuitable. It may terminate the indefinite suspension of a member of a Subordinate Lodge, for non-payment of dues, and upon reversal of the decision of a Subordinate, may reinstate a suspended or expelled member, without consent of his Lodge.—(*Vol.* 2. *p.* 178, 205, 208, 349.)

§5. The officers of a Grand Lodge are Most Worthy Grand Master, Right Worthy Deputy Grand Master, R. W. G. Warden, R. W. G. Secretary, R. W. G. Treasurer, who are elected; Worthy Grand Marshal, W. G. Conductor, W. G. Guardian, who are appointed by the Grand Master.

§6. The Most Worthy Grand Master has powers and duties prescribed in the charge books of the Order, and performs such duties as are imposed upon him by his Grand Lodge. He has supervisory power over the Order, and must check the introduction of subjects foreign to the purposes of the Order. He has not power, by virtue of his office to grant dispensations for opening Lodges, but it is competent for his Grand Lodge to confer such power upon him. He is required to enforce the law suppressing the publication of the work, cards and diplomas, as directed by the G. L. U. S. If he or his Grand Lodge grant permission to a Lodge to apply for relief, he furnishes written authority according to the form in the appendix. He may visit Subordinates, examine their books, and install their officers. He may introduce visiting brethren into any Lodge within his jurisdiction, without the usual examination.—(*Vol.* 2. *p.* 302, 315, 352.—*Hopkins D.*, 2 *series*, *No.* 41.—*By-Laws*, *Art.* 17.)

§7. The other elective officers have powers and duties as prescribed in the charge books; and have the power to introduce visiting brethren within the jurisdiction of their Grand Lodge.—(*By-Laws*, *Art* 17.)

§8. The appointed officers have duties as prescribed in the charge books of the Order.

§9. A Grand Lodge has power to expel a member from its own body, but it possesses no power to expel a member altogether from the Order. It may, however, order a Subordinate Lodge to try a member, and to this order the Subordinate must yield obedience.—(*Vol.* 2, *p.* 485.)

ARTICLE III.—Subordinate Lodges.

§1. Subordinate Lodges derive their powers from the authority which created them, and are restricted to the exercise of those conferred by their warrants and the laws of the several Grand Lodges under which they exist. They have no legislative power whatever except to make By-Laws for their own internal government.

§2. They are subject at all times to the supervision and control of their Grand Lodges, and for any violation or neglect of their duties, may be punished as the Grand Lodge may determine. They must receive with respect all communications emanating from their superiors.—(*Vol.* 2, *p.* 208.)

§3. They have no authority to ask advice or counsel from any other quarter than the Grand Lodge by which they are governed, nor can they lawfully enter into correspondence with each other, without the consent and approval of their Grand Lodges.

§4. Subordinate Lodges under the jurisdiction of the Grand Lodge of the United States, may adopt a Constitution, subject to the approval of the Grand Lodge of the United States; they make semi-yearly and annual returns to that body, transmitting therewith their dues, being ten per centum on their receipts; and each Subordinate Lodge is furnished with a printed copy of the proceedings of the G. L. U. S.—(*Cons. Art. XII, By-Laws, Art.* 3, 10, 11, 21.)

§5. A Subordinate Lodge under the jurisdiction of the Grand Lodge of the United States, which fails to make its returns for one year forfeits its charter.—(*Vol.* 2, *p.* 76, 88.)

§6. The location of a Subordinate Lodge is designated in its charter, and it cannot remove but with the sanction of its Grand Lodge. It may select its own place of meeting, and its Grand Lodge cannot interfere with such selection, if the Lodge-room be private and safe from intrusion.—(*Vol.* 2, *p.* 55, 178, 208.)

§7. The charter of a Subordinate Lodge cannot be surrendered by a majority of its members, but remains in force so long as five members are willing to work under it.— (*Vol.* 1, *p.* 370.)

§8. When a charter of a Subordinate Lodge has been surrendered or reclaimed, its books and effects must be placed in the keeping of the Grand Lodge; and its charter, name, number, and property cannot be restored to any but a sufficient number of its original members.—(*Vol.* 1, *p.* 53, 311.)

§9. No person is eligible to membership in any Subordinate Lodge, under the jurisdiction of the Grand Lodge of the United States, or of the Grand Lodge of British North America, or of any of the Grand Lodges, by either of said supreme bodies established, except he be a free white male, of good moral character, of the age of twenty-one years, and a believer in a Supreme Being, the Creator and Preserver of the Universe.—(*Vol.* 2, *p.* 54, 55, 329.)

§10. No person can hold membership in more than one Subordinate Lodge at the same time.—(*By-Laws, Art.* 15, *vol.* 1, *p.* 245.)

§11. A Subordinate Lodge is not allowed to initiate a person at a place remote from his residence, if a Lodge be located in his immediate neighborhood.—(*By-Laws, Art. 30, vol. 2, p.* 475, 497.)

§12. It cannot under any circumstances confer honorary membership, nor admit a person without payment of fee, except under regulations of its Grand Lodge.—(*Vol.2, p.* 61, 207.)

§13. Good standing signifies contributing membership in a Subordinate Lodge, and freedom from any disability by reason of non-payment of dues, or of charges under the penal provisions of the Lodge.—(*Vol.* 1, *p.* 547.)

§14. A member of a Subordinate Lodge, may on his own written application, withdraw from the Order, without a withdrawal card.—(*Vol.* 2, *p.* 201.)

§15. The officers of a Subordinate Lodge are the N. G., V. G., Secretary, Permanent Secretary (if necessary) and Treasurer, who are elected by the Lodge ; Warden, Conductor, O. G., I. G., R. and L. S. of N. G., R. and L. S. of V. G., R. S. S., L. S. S., who are appointed by the N. G.— (*Usage.*)

§16. They have duties and powers as prescribed by the charge books of the Order, and the laws of the Grand Lodge, under which they exist. The N. G. and V. G., are entitled to the T. P. W., and superintend the examination of visitors.—(*Vol.* 2, *p.* 86.)

§17. Twenty-six nights service as an inferior officer is a sufficient qualification for the office of V. G., provided the brother has attained to sufficient degrees, and is otherwise competent.—(*Vol.* 2, *p.* 463.)

§18. Service for one term in the V. G.'s chair is a necessary qualification for the office of N. G.—(*Vol.* 2, *p.* 467.)

§19. In the absence of the N. G., it is not only the right, but the duty of the V. G., to take the place of the superior officer, and fulfil all his functions.—(*Vol.* 2, *p.* 464.)

§20. Service as N. G. for a full term, or the remnant of a term by filling a vacancy, or a majority of nights of a regular term, if a new Lodge be instituted in the course thereof, entitles a brother to the rank of P. G., and to a seat in his Grand Lodge.—(*Vol.* 2, *p.* 45, 191.)

§21. The Past official degrees of N. G., V. G. and Secretary, are conferred upon brothers who have discharged the duties of those offices, by their Grand Lodge. The first N. G. of a new Lodge is entitled to the official degrees, and the first V. G. to the degrees of P. V. G. and P. Secretary, but in no other case can they be conferred, except for service actually performed.—(*Vol.* 2, *p.* 191, 479.)

§22. The officers of a Subordinate Lodge are installed according to the form prescribed by the Grand Lodge of the United Sates by the Grand Master, or by a Deputy by him appointed. The Grand Master retains the privilege of in stalling the officers of any Lodge if he deem proper.—(*Vol.* 2, *p.* 315 ; *By-Laws, Art.* 27.)

§23. The terms of Subordinate Lodges are six months each, commencing on the first meeting of July and the first meeting of January in each year.—(*Vol.* 2, *p.* 296, 308.)

§24. In case of a Subordinate Lodge, instituted before the expiration of a term, if fourteen weeks remain, they shall be deemed a regular term ; if less than that number of weeks remain, the remnant is added to the ensuing term, and the officers serve until the close thereof.—(*Vol.* 2, *p.* 190.)

§25. If a member of a Subordinate Lodge refuse to stand trial upon charges duly preferred, he cannot in his absence be tried, but may be expelled for contempt.—(*Vol.* 2, *p.* 202.)

§26. If a member acknowledge his guilt upon charges preferred, the penalty may be imposed without trial.—(*Ibid.*)

§27. Upon the trial of a member charged, an exparte statement cannot be introduced as testimony ; his wife cannot be permitted to testify ; but all evidence tending to a fair investigation of his case may be admitted.—(*Vol.* 2, *p.* 51.)

§28. Indefinite suspension of a member for non-payment of dues, may be terminated by a Grand Lodge without the consent of its Subordinate.—*Vol.* 2, *p.* 205-6.)

§29. Suspension of membership by act of a Lodge as a

means of punishment, works no suspension of arrears, but the arrears run on during the time of the suspension.—(*General Usage.*)

§30. A new trial of a member of a Subordinate Lodge, cannot be ordered by a Grand Lodge, in case of appeal, on the ground of informality, or want of fairness on the former trial, unless such facts, or the discovery of new testimony be proved.—(*Vol.* 2, *p.* 213.)

§31. If upon an appeal of a member of the Subordinate Lodge, the Grand Lodge reverses the decision of its Subordinate, the brother charged may be reinstated without the consent of the Subordinate Lodge.—(*Vol.* 2, *p.* 349.)

§32. A member of a Subordinate Lodge, except it be under the immediate jurisdiction of the Grand Lodge of the United States, cannot appeal to that body.—(*Vol.* 1, *p.* 36, 130, *vol.* 2, *p.* 146, *approved usage.*)

§33. Pending an appeal of a Subordinate Lodge, to the Grand Lodge of the United States, an individual under penalty, and whose case is involved in the appeal, occupies the position prescribed for him by his Grand Lodge.—*Vol.* 2, *p.* 299.)

§34. A Subordinate Lodge cannot appeal to the Grand Lodge of the United States, unless with the consent of its Grand Lodge, except in case of its expulsion, it having first surrendered its effects.—(*Cons. Art. 1, as amended, vol.* 2, *p.* 145.)

§35. If a member of a Subordinate Lodge commit suicide, his family are nevertheless entitled to the funeral benefits. —(*Vol.* 2, *p.* 205.)

§36. A Subordinate Lodge can ask for relief only through its Grand Lodge or Grand Master, and it must obtain the prescribed certificate from such authority.—(*Vol.* 2, *p.* 256, 302, *see appendix.*)

§37. Subordinate Lodges and members thereof are prohibited from printing any of the lectures, charges, odes, diplomas, &c., adopted and printed by the Grand Lodge of the United States.—(*Vol.* 2, *p.* 352.)

§38. Lectures, unless authorized by the regulations of the local jurisdictions, are prohibited in Subordinate Lodges. —(*Vol.* 2, *p.* 57.)

§39. Visiting and withdrawal cards of the prescribed forms, are given to members in good standing upon application therefor.—(*Vol. 2, p. 74, 75.*)

§40. Upon granting a withdrawal card to a member upon application, his membership ceases at once, whether the card be taken or not.—(*Vol. 2, p. 312.*)

§41. If a Lodge grant relief to a travelling brother, the amount of benefit granted is endorsed upon his card.—(*Vol. 2, p. 299.*)

§42. Whenever a Lodge becomes extinct, its members may receive from the Grand Recording Secretary, certificates of their regular connexion, in order to enable them to join other Lodges.—(*Vol. 1, p. 458, vol. 2, p. 455.*)

§43. There is no reason for refusing to receive into the American Order, persons who have *withdrawn* from the Manchester Unity; but there being no communion between that body and the Grand Lodge of the United States, such persons can only come in by *initiation*, and precisely as other initiates do.—(*Vol. 2, p. 470.*)

§44. A Lodge working in a foreign language, may keep a record of its proceedings in the language in which it works; but it is bound also to keep a record in the English language.—(*Vol. 2, p. 509.*

§45. The junior P. G. is not strictly an officer of the Lodge, but it is his duty to occupy the seat of Past Grand for one term, and deliver the Past Grand's charge at initiation. It is therefore improper that he should be elected to any office.—(*Vol. 2, p. 509.*)

§46. The order of business contained in the printed work of Subordinates is to be considered in the light of a recommendation merely. If the Subordinates can conveniently adhere to the form in the charge book, it is only proper that they should do so; if they cannot, they may regulate the order of business to suit their particular necessities.—(*Vol. 2, p. 460.*)

ARTICLE IV.—DEGREE LODGES AND DEGREES.

§1. The legality of Degree Lodges is recognized by the Grand Lodge of the United States.—(*Vol. 2, p. 347.*)

§2. The price for Degrees is left to the control of the local Grand Lodges.—(*Vol* 2, *p.* 207.)

§3. No Lodge can confer Degrees upon a member of another Lodge, but with the consent of the Lodge to which the member belongs.—(*By-Laws*, *Art.* 15.(

§3. If the preceding law be violated, the Lodge conferring the Degrees shall pay the amount of fees to the Lodge of which the recipient of the degrees was a member.— (*Vol.* 1, *p.* 274.)

§4. The time, place and manner of conferring the Subordinate Degrees are proper subjects for local legislation. But under no circumstances would it be lawful to permit members to vote on applications for degrees, who have not received the degree applied for.—(*Vol* 2, *p.* 487.)

§5. The Grand Encampment degree can regularly be given, only during the session, and in the room in which the Grand Encampment is assembled, but by special permission it may be conferred in some contiguous room.— (*Vol.* 2, *p.* 487.)

§6. A similar rule applies to the Grand Lodge degree.— (*Vol.* 2, *p.* 487.)

§7. Grand Lodges may authorize District Deputy Grand Masters to confer the *Past Official* degrees at any time, upon persons duly qualified, or may authorize said degrees to be conferred in any other manner.—(*Vol.* 2, *p.* 487.)

5*

DIVISION FOURTH.

ARTICLE I.—Grand Encampments.

Origin, Organization, Powers.

§1. Grand Encampments exist by virtue of warrants or dispensations duly granted or confirmed by the Grand Lodge of the United States. Upon all occasions when precedence is to be observed, they rank below State Grand Lodges, which are the supreme legislative heads within their respective jurisdictions.—(*Cons. Art.* 1; *By-Laws, Art.* 4, 13, *vol.* 1, *p.* 456.)

§2. They consist of all Past Chief Patriarchs or Past High Priests, or if their Constitutions so determine, of all Past Chief Patriarchs only, within their respective jurisdictions, but no person can be a member of more than one G. Encampment at the same time.—(*Vol.* 1, *p.* 355, *vol.* 2, *p.* 56, 354, *By-Laws, Art.* 15, *vol.* 2, *p.* 510.)

§3. They work in the Grand Encampment Degree.— (*Vol.* 1, *p.* 447–50.)

§4. Each Grand Encampment has a seal, an impression whereof in wax is sent to the Grand Recording Secretary; it adopts a Constitution subject to the approval of the G. Lodge of the United States; makes to that body an annual return, is entitled to a Representative, and if containing within its jurisdiction more than one thousand members, two Representatives in the Grand Lodge of the United States; it must pay for each vote to which it is entitled twenty dollars per annum, but it cannot vote by its Representative if it be more than one year in arrears for dues to the Grand Lodge of the United States. It may nominate by its Representative or Representatives, a candidate for the office of Grand Sire, and a candidate for the office of Deputy Grand Sire; it must pay the expenses of its Representative, furnish him with a certificate in proper form, and with all documents necessary in the discharge of the duties of his office; it is entitled to such number of copies of the

54

printed proceedings of the Grand Lodge of the United States, as it has Subordinates in its jurisdiction, for its own use and an equal number to be distributed among such Subordinates.—(*Cons. Art.* 10, 12, 14, *By-Laws, Art.* 9, 10, 11, 12, 19, 21.)

§5. Grand Encampments are required to enforce upon their Subordinates a strict adherence to the prescribed work; they must not use, nor suffer to be used any other than the prescribed charges, lectures, degrees, ceremonies, forms of installation and regalia, and they are held responsible for any irregularities in this respect, which they allow under their jurisdictions.—(*By-Laws, Art.* 23.)

§6. They must enact laws to prohibit their Subordinates from initiating brethren from other States, or at places remote from their permanent residence, if such reridence be in the neighborhood of an Encampment.—(*By-Laws, Art.* 30.)

§7. Each Grand Encampment has control over all Subordinate Encampments within its jurisdiction. It has power to grant charters and to open Encampments; it enacts laws for the government of its Subordinates, prescribing the forms of their returns, and requires of them the payment of dues to defray its expenses.—(*Usage.*)

§8. It receives appeals from its Subordinates and their members, and none except an expelled Subordinate Encampment, which has surrendered its effects, can appeal but with its consent, from its decision to the Grand Lodge of the United States.—(*Cons. Art.* 1.)

§9. It enforces its laws upon its Subordinates. It may for cause annul the Charter of a Subordinate Encampment. In case of the forfeiture or annulment of a charter it takes possession of the books and effects of the Subordinate, but it cannot restore these, nor the name and number of the Subordinate to any persons except the former members.—(*Usage.*)

§10. The officers of a Grand Encampment are, M. W. Grand Patriarch, M. E. Grand High Priest, R. W. Grand Senior Warden, R. W. G. Scribe, R. W. G. Treasurer, R. W. Junior Warden, who are elected, and G. Sentinel, who is appointed by the G. P.

§11. The Grand Patriarch has powers and duties as prescribed in the charge books of the Order; he has supervisory authority over the jurisdiction of his Grand Encampment; he may introduce visiting brethren into any
Encampment within his jurisdiction, to which they would
be entitled to visit by card.—(*Usage—P. G. S. Hopkins*,
2d Ser. Letters, **54**.)

§12. The other elective officers have powers and duties
as prescribed in the charge books, and may introduce visiting brethren without examination, into any Encampment
within the jurisdiction of their Grand Encampment.

ARTICLE II.—SUBORDINATE ENCAMPMENTS.

§1. Subordinate Encampmen's exist by virtue of warrants or charters, duly granted by the competent authority within whose jurisdiction they are established, and are
subject to their superior, with the same restrictions and
prohibitions before prescribed for Subordinate Lodges.—
(*By-Laws, Art. 2.*)

§2. Subordinate Encampments under the jurisdiction of
the Grand Lodge of the United States, may adopt Constitutions subject to the approval of that Body; they must
transmit to the Grand Lodge of the United States semi-
annual returns, accompanied by their dues, viz: ten per
centum on their receipts, and failing to make returns
for one year their charters are forfeited. In case of the
establishment of a Grand Encampment in the State, District or Territory in which they are located, they pass under the jurisdiction of such Grand Encampment.—(*Cons.
Art.* 12—*By-Laws, Art.* 4, 10, 16; *vol.* 2, *p.* 76, 88.)

§3. If the number of members of a Subordinate be reduced below its constitutional quorum, viz: seven members,
its charter is forfeited, and its books and effects must be
surrendered to the Grand Body under which it exists; and
its name, number, charter and property will be restored to
none, save its orginal members.—(*Vol.* 1, *p.* 370, *vol.* 2, *p.*
195.)

§4. If a Subordinate Encampment created by the Grand
Lodge of the United States, has become extinct, and sub-

sequently a Grand Encampment be established in the State, District or Territory, within which it was located, a sufficient number of the original members of the Subordinate may with the consent of such Grand Encampment, apply to the Grand Lodge of the United States for a restoration of its charter and effects.—*(Vol. 2, p. 195.)*

§5. To acquire or retain membership in an Encampment full membership in a Subordinate Lodge is indispensably necessary.—*(Vol. 2, p. 350.)*

§6. No person can hold membership in more than one Encampment at the same time.—*(By-Laws, Art. 15.)*

§7. The granting of a withdrawal card by a Subordinate Lodge to one of its members who is also a member of an Encampment, has the effect of severing at once his connection with his Encampment, but on the renewal of his membership in a Subordinate Lodge his membership in his Encampment is thereby renewed, provided such renewal shall occur within one month from the date of such withdrawal card.—*(Vol. 2, p. 352.)*

§8. By the renewal of membership in a Subordinate Lodge (within the time limited,) membership in the Encampment is *ipso facto* renewed, and if the Patriarch desires to *withdraw,* he must pursue the usual course.—*(Vol. 2, p. 454.)*

§9. Where by the operation of the law as set forth in §7, a Patriarch loses his membership in an Encampment, it is the duty of the proper officers of such Encampment to furnish said Patriarch with a regular withdrawal card, provided said Patriarch shall be in good standing and comply with the regulations of said Encampment touching such cards.—*(Vol. 2, p. 461.)*

§10. Subordinate Encampments are prohibited from initiating brethren at places remote from their residence while Encampments are located in the neighborhood of such residence.—*(By-Laws, Art. 30.)*

§11. A member of an Encampment may withdraw therefrom, if free from charge, without taking a card.—*(Vol. 2, p. 201.)*

§12. A member under charges in an Encampment, if he

plead guilty, may receive his penalty without trial; if he refuse to appear he may be punished for contempt.—(*Vol.* 2, *p.* 201–2.

§13. The terms of Subordinate Encampments are six months, ending with June and December of each year. In case of a new Encampment, if there be more than thirteen weeks between the time of its institution and the termination of the regular term, they are considered a full term; if there be thirteen weeks or less, then the same, with the ensuing term, constitute one term.—(*Vol.* 1, *p.* 451; *vol.* 2, *p.* 190.)

§14. The officers of an Encampment are, Chief Patriarch, High Priest, Senior Warden, Scribe, Treasurer, Junior Warden, who are elected by the Encampment, Guide, Sentinel, 1st, 2d, 3d, 4th Watches, who are appointed by the C. P., 1st and 2d G. of T., who are appointed by the H. P.

§15. The duties of the C. P. are prescribed in the charge books. He is entitled to the T. P. W., and superintends and directs the examination of visiting brethren.—(*Vol.* 2, *p.* 300, 338.)

§16. The duties of the other officers are contained in the charge books of the Order. The S. W. is entitled to the T. P. W.

§17. The business of an Encampment must not be allowed to interfere with the business of any Lodge.—(*Vol.* 1, *p.* 241.)

§18. The Encampment regalia, except by visitors, can be worn only in an Encampment, but members of a Grand Lodge who have received the R. P. Degree, may wear the colors of the Encampment in Grand Lodge.—(*Vol.* 1, *p.* 242, *By-Laws, Art.* 25, 31.

§19. It is discretionary with the Encampments to use prayer, or not, at the *opening and closing.* *In the conferring of the degrees,* the prayers are an integral part of the work and cannot be omitted.—(*Vol.* 2, *p.* 428–9.)

§20. The J. W. may preside in the absence of the C. P. and S. W., if the local laws do not prohibit it.—(*Vol.* 2, *p.* 509.)

§21. In the absence of the H. P., if no P. H. P. be present, any R. P. member may perform all the duties of that officer, if the local laws do not prohibit it.—(*Vol.* 2, *p.* 509.)

APPENDIX I.

CONSTITUTION.

WHEREAS, it is of great importance that those instituti· should be perpetuated which are of essential benef mankind; *and whereas*, Odd-Fellowship is based upon the eternal principles of universal Friendship, Philanthropy and Beneficence—*Therefore*, the Grand Lodge of the United States of the Independent Order of Odd-Fellows, to bind the Order more effectually in a common and indissoluble union : to provide for its best interests and to secure to all time the advantages and blessings which it dispenses, doth ordain and establish this CONSTITUTION.

Done in the City of Baltimore, in the State of Maryland, this fifth day of September, in the year one thousand eight hundred and thirty-three.

ARTICLE I.

This Lodge shall be known by the name, style and title of the "Grand Lodge of the United States of the Independent Order of Odd-Fellows," and possesses original and exclusive jurisdiction in Odd-Fellowship, over the territories comprising the Federal Government of the United States. It is the source of all true and legitimate authority in Odd-Fellowship in the United States of America. All State, District and Territorial Grand Lodges and Encampments assemble under its warrant, and derive their authority from it. With it is placed the power to enact such laws and regulations as shall be for the good of the Order in general. It is the ultimate tribunal to which all matters of general importance to the State, District and Territo-

59

rial Grand Lodges and Grand Encampments are to be referred, and its decisions thereon shall be final and conclusive. With the consent of the Grand Lodge or Grand Encampment of a State, District or Territory, it may receive an appeal of a Subordinate Lodge or Encampment, from the decision of a Grand Lodge or Grand Encampment; such consent, however, not being necessary when an expelled Lodge or Encampment, after having delivered up its effects, appeals from the decision of its Grand Lodge or Grand Encampment. To it belongs the power to regulate and control the work of the Order, and the several degrees belonging thereto; and to fix and determine the customs and usages, in regard to all things which concern Odd-Fellowship. It has inherent power to establish Lodges or Encampments in foreign countries where no Grand Lodge and Grand Encampment exists. Such Lodges and Encampments shall work by virtue of a warrant granted by this Grand Lodge.

ARTICLE II.

§1. The members of this Grand Lodge shall be, the Grand Sire, Deputy Grand Sire, Grand Recording Secretary, Grand Corresponding Secretary, Grand Treasurer, Grand Marshal, Grand Guardian, Grand Chaplain, and the Representatives from State, District, and Territorial Grand Lodges and Grand Encampments, acting under legal, unreclaimed warrants granted by this Grand Lodge.

ARTICLE III.

The elective officers shall be, Most Worthy Grand Sire, Right Worthy D. G. Sire, Grand Recording Secretary, G. Corresponding Secretary, and Grand Treasurer, all of whom shall be elected biennially, at the stated meetings of this G. Lodge, in September, except the Grand Corresponding Secretary, who shall be elected during the pleasure of this G. Lodge. They shall be duly installed, and enter on the duties of their offices at the stated meeting next ensuing their election. The Right Worthy Grand Marshal, Right Worthy G. Guardian, and Right Worthy G. Chaplain, shall be nominated by the Grand Sire, and if approved of by the G. Lodge, they shall be installed at the stated meeting next ensuing the election of Grand Officers. If, however, any of the elective officers fail to appear to be installed at the time provided, the particular office or offices shall be declared vacant, and the Grand Lodge shall, in that event, proceed to a new election to fill such vacancy or vacancies, and the officer or officers so elected shall be accordingly installed. They shall attend each meeting of the Grand Lodge, and perform such other duties as are enjoined by the laws and regulations of the ¡Order, and such as may be required by the presiding officer. No officer (who is not also a Representative) shall be permitted to vote; except the Grand Sire, in case of equal division.

Article IV.

The Grand Sire shall preside at all meetings of the Grand Lodge, preserve order, and enforce the laws thereof. He shall have the casting vote whenever the Lodge shall be equally divided; but shall not vote on any other occasion. During the recess of this Grand Lodge he shall have a general superintendence over the interests of the Order, and make report to the next stated meeting of his acts and doings in relation thereto. He shall not hold any office in any State, District or Territorial Grand Lodge or Grand Encampment, while acting as Grand Sire.

Article V.

§1. The Deputy Grand Sire shall open and close the meetings of the Grand Lodge, support the Grand Sire by his advice and assistance, and preside in his absence.

§2. In the absence of the Grand Sire and Deputy Grand Sire, the Grand Lodge shall elect a Grand Sire *pro tempore.*

Article VI.

§1. The G. Recording Secretary shall make a just and true record of all the proceedings of the Grand Lodge in a book provided for that purpose; summon the members to attend at stated and special meetings ; keep accounts between the Grand Lodge and the Grand and Subordinate Lodges and Encampments under its jurisdiction ; read all petitions, reports and communications ; and perform such other duties as the Grand Lodge may from time to time require. He shall receive for his services such sum of money as the Grand Lodge shall from time to time determine.

§2. The Grand Corresponding Secretary shall write all letters and communications, carry on, under the direction of the Grand Lodge or Grand Sire, its correspondence, and transact such business of this Grand Lodge, appertaining to his office, as may be required of him by the Grand Lodge. All communications transmitted or received by him, shall be laid before the Grand Lodge

Article VII.

The Grand Treasurer shall keep the moneys of the G. Lodge, and pay all orders drawn on him by the Grand Sire, attested by the Grand Secretary, under the seal of the Grand Lodge. He shall lay before the Grand Lodge, at its stated meeting in September, a full and correct statement of his accounts.

Article VIII.

Past Grand Sires shall be admitted to seats in this Grand Lodge, and be entitled to vote on all questions coming before the Grand Lodge, provided they be not Representatives.

Article IX.

The Grand Guardian shall prove every brother before he admits him, and allow no one to depart without the password.

Article X.

Representatives from Grand Lodges and Grand Encampments must be Past Grands in good standing, who have received the R. P. Degree. They must be elected or appointed by the Grand Lodge or Grand Encampment they represent, for the term of two years from the commencement of the annual session of the Grand Lodge of the United States, preceding which they shall have been so elected or appointed, and must be furnished with a certificate, as follows:

F. L. and T.

To the R. W. Grand Lodge of the United States of the I. O. of O. F.

This certifies that P. G. ———— ————, has been duly elected (or appointed) Representative from the Grand Lodge, (or Grand Encampment) of ————, to the Grand Lodge of the United States.

Witness our hands and the Seal of the Grand ————, this ———— day of ————

SEAL

———— ————, G. Master (or G. Patriarch.)
———— ————, G. Secretary, (or G. Scribe.)

No brother shall represent a Grand Lodge or Grand Encampment in this Grand Lodge, unless he resides in the State, District or Territory where the Grand Lodge or G. Encampment of which he offers himself as a Representative is located. No Representative shall represent more than one Grand Body at the same time.

The Representatives shall be entitled to vote on all questions before the Grand-Lodge, in the manner following, to wit: Each Grand Lodge or Grand Encampment having less than one thousand members, one vote; and each Grand Lodge or Grand Encampment having more than one thousand members, one additional vote; the annual returns of the several Grand Lodges and Grand Encampments to determine the number of votes which each Grand Lodge or Grand Encampment is entitled to.

ARTICLE XI.

The Grand Lodge of the United States shall meet annually on the third Monday in September. It may meet on its own adjournments; and *specially*, on the call of the Grand Sire. When the purpose of meeting is the granting of a charter, the Grand Sire may convene the Grand Lodge, first causing two weeks notice to be given to the Representatives of the different Grand Lodges and Grand Encampments, and communicating to them the special purpose thereof. In other special cases, the Grand Sire shall cause two months notice to be given to the different State, District and Territorial Grand Lodges and Grand Encampments, communicating to them the purpose for which the special meeting is called. In no case shall any business be transacted at a special meeting, unless notice thereof has been given as above stated. The hour of meeting shall be nine o'clock, A. M., and at such place as the Grand Lodge shall from time to time determine.

ARTICLE XII.

The revenue of the Grand Lodge shall be as follows:

1st. Fees for Grand Lodge or Grand Encampment charter, $30.

2d. Fees for charter for Subordinate Lodges or Encampments, working under its immediate jurisdiction, $30.

3rd. Dues from Subordinate Lodges or Encampments, holding warrants from this Lodge, 10 per cent. on their receipts.

4th. Dues from State, District or Territorial Grand Lodges and Grand Encampments, $20 per annum, for each vote they shall be entitled to in this Lodge.

ARTICLE XIII.

In case of death, resignation, disqualification, or refusal of the Grand Sire to serve, the duties of the office shall be performed by the R. W. D. G. Sire until the next stated meeting of the Grand Lodge, when an election shall be had for Grand Sire. In case of the death, resignation, disqualification, or refusal to serve of any elective or appointed officer, the Grand Sire shall appoint some qualified brother to perform the duties until the next stated meeting, when an election or appointment, as the case may require, shall take place.

ARTICLE XIV.

Each Grand Lodge, and each Grand Encampment working under an unreclaimed warrant granted by the Grand

Lodge of the United States, may by its Representative, nominate a candidate for the office of Grand Sire and a candidate for the office of Deputy Grand Sire. The candidate thus nominated must be a Past Grand Master, who shall have received the R. P. Degree, and be a contributing member of a Subordinate Lodge. A majority of all the votes given shall be necessary to elect a Grand Sire or Deputy Grand Sire.

Article XV.

A majority of the Representatives of the several Grand Lodges and Grand Encampments shall be necessary to form a quorum for the transaction of business. All questions, except as hereafter provided, shall be decided by a majority of the votes given.

Article XVI.

With the consent and approval, from time to time expressed, of this Grand Lodge, the Most Worthy Grand Sire may accredit any officer or member of this Grand Lodge as a special Grand Representative, near the Grand Lodge of any sovereign jurisdiction in Odd-Fellowship, recognized by this Grand Lodge , and in such case the necessary expenses of such special Grand Representative's visit may be appropriated for from the funds of this Grand Lodge And any officer or member of any such foreign Grand Lodge, who may be duly accredited from the same as a special Grand Representative near this Grand Lodge, shall be admitted to a seat or the floor of this Grand Lodge, and shall have a deliberative voice, but not a vote in the proceedings of this G L —(*Adopted session* 1847)

Article XVII.

By-Laws, in conformity with this Constitution, may be made, which shall not be altered or amended, unless such amendment be made at a stated meeting, and be assented to by two-thirds of the votes given.

Article XVIII.

Any alteration or amendment of this Constitution must be offered to this Grand Lodge, in writing, at a stated meeting thereof, and if seconded, it shall be entered on the minutes : at the next stated meeting the amendments may be considered, and if agreed to by two-thirds of the votes given, shall become a part of the Constitution.

BY-LAWS.

ARTICLE I.

Upon the petition of five brothers of the Order, in good standing, praying for a charter to open a Subordinate Lodge in a State, District or Territory, where a Grand Lodge has not been established, this Lodge may Grant the same. All Subordinate Lodges receiving warrants from the Grand Lodge of the United States, shall be opened by a Past Grand of the Order, regularly deputized therefor by the Grand Sire, who shall deliver to such Lodge the warrant and charge books, and shall at the opening thereof give all necessary instruction. Such Lodge shall be visited, at least once a year, by the Grand Sire, or some Past Grand deputized by him for that purpose, or by a D. D. Grand Sire.

ARTICLE II.

Upon the petition of seven qualified members of the Order, in good standing, praying for a warrant to open an Encampment in a State, District or Territory, where a Grand Encampment has not been established, this Lodge may grant the same. All Encampments receiving warrants from this Grand Lodge shall be opened by the Grand Sire, or by a qualified Patriarch, who shall deliver to such Encampment the warrant and charge books, and such instructions as may be necessary. Such Encampment shall be visited, at least once a year, by the Grand Sire, District Deputy Grand Sire, or by some Patriarch deputized by him for that purpose.

ARTICLE III.

Subordinate Lodges and Encampments, working immediately under the jurisdiction of this Grand Lodge, shall transmit to the Grand Recording Secretary quarterly reports, containing the same information as is required from Grand

66

Lodges and Encampments by Article XI of these laws. The reports shall be accompanied by the dues in current money.

ARTICLE IV.

Three or more Subordinate Lodges or Encampments, located in any State, District or Territory, (where a Grand Lodge or Grand Encampment has not been established,) having seven Past Grands or Past C. Patriarchs, in good standing, may petition the Grand Lodge of the United States, in writing, praying for the charter of a Grand Lodge or Grand Encampment, in such State, District or Territory, which if approved of by a majority of the votes given, shall be granted; and such Grand Lodge or Grand Encampment shall be opened by the Grand Sire, or some qualified brother or Patriarch, whom he shall deputize for that purpose.

ARTICLE V.

All applications for Charters for Grand Lodges or Grand Encampments, must be by a vote of a majority of the Lodges or Encampments within the State, District or Territory, as follows: When three or more Lodges or Encampments shall agree in the opinion that a Grand Lodge or Grand Encampment will contribute to the general interest, notice thereof shall be given to all the Lodges or Encampments in the State, District or Territory, inviting them to meet in consultation, at some convenient time and place. Each Lodge or Encampment shall appoint one or more of its Past Grands or Past Chief Patriarchs, or Past High Priests, as Representatives, to meet in Convention and consider the propriety of applying for a Grand Charter, as well as to determine upon the place for the erection of the Grand Lodge or Encampment, (both of which questions shall be decided by a majority vote, which majority vote must represent at least three Lodges or Encampments.) Should any Lodge or Encampment neglect or refuse to send a Representative, or should the Representative, from accident or other cause, fail to attend, it shall not operate to defeat

the proceedings of such as may assemble, provided a sufficient number be present to comply with the preceding requirements. Each Subordinate Lodge or Encampment
shall furnish to its Representative a statement, under the
seal of the Lodge or Encampment, of the number of Past
Grands or Past Chief Patriarchs, in good standing, belonging to it. At the meeting of these Representatives the votes
shall be by Lodges or Encampments, and the application
shall be in the following form, to wit:

To the R. W. Grand Lodge of the United
States of the I. O. of O. F.

The petition of ———— Lodge, (or Encampment,) No. 1,
———— No. 2, ———— No 3, of ———— respectfully represents, that at present they work under warrants granted by
your R. W. body ; that at present they have ———— Past
Grands, (or Past C. Patriarchs) in good standing. They
are of opinion that it would be of advantage to the Order,
to establish a Grand Lodge, (or Grand Encampment) in the
————. They therefore pray your R. W. body to grant
a charter for a Grand Lodge (or Grand Encampment) in
the ————, to be located at ————.

Witness our hands and seals this —— day of ——, 18—.

A. B., Representative of No. 1.
C. D., Representative of No. 2.
E. F., Representative of No. 3.

ARTICLE VI.

All travelling and other expenses of the Grand Sire, Past
Grand or Patriarch, deputized by him to open a Grand or
Subordinate Lodge or Encampment, shall be paid by such
Lodge or Encampment.

ARTICLE VII.

Applications for Grand or Subordinate Lodges or Encampments must be accompanied by the fee for the same,
which shall be returned if the charter is not granted.

ARTICLE VIII.

No more than one Grand Lodge or Grand Encampment
shall be chartered in any State, District or Territory.

ARTICLE IX.

Each Grand Lodge and Grand Encampment shall have a Seal, an impression whereof in wax shall be sent to the Grand Secretary, and be deposited in the archives of the Grand Lodge of the United States.

ARTICLE X.

The Constitution of each Grand and Subordinate Lodge or Encampment, chartered by this Grand Lodge, immediately on its adoption, shall be forwarded to this Grand Lodge for its approval.

ARTICLE XI.

Annual returns shall be made by each State, District or Territorial Grand Lodge or Grand Encampment, in which they shall give full information of the number of members in good standing, names of Grand Officers, Past Grand Officers, number of initiations, rejections, suspensions and cause, expulsions and cause, admissions by card, withdrawals by card, deaths, amount expended for relief of brothers, amount expended for education of orphans, and whole amount of receipts; forms for which shall be furnished by this Grand Lodge. Said returns shall be made to the Grand Recording Secretary, at least one month previous to the annual meeting of this body, and shall be accompanied with the dues thereon in money current at par in the place where the meeting of this body is held.

ARTICLE XII.

No Grand Lodge or Grand Encampment which shall be in arrears more than one year for dues to this Grand Lodge, shall be allowed to vote by its Representative, or Representatives.

ARTICLE XIII.

During the recess of the Grand Lodge of the United States, the Grand Sire, Deputy Grand Sire, and Grand Recording Secretary shall be authorized to grant dispensations to open Grand Lodges or Encampments, or Subordinate Lodges or Encampments, which shall be submitted to this Grand Lodge for approval and confirmation at its next annual meeting.

ARTICLE XIV.

The Grand Sire shall, through the Grand Representatives, at each session of the Grand Lodge, forward immediately, a travelling password to the Grand Master of each Grand Lodge, the Grand Patriarch of each Grand Encampment, and to the N. G's of Subordinate Lodges, and the C. P's of Encampments working under this jurisdiction; and the Grand Master and Grand Patriarch shall communicate the same to the N. G's of the several Lodges, and the C. P's of Encampments in the State, District, or Territory. The said T. P. W. to go into operation on the first day of January in each and every year.

ARTICLE XV.

No person shall hold membership in more than one Grand or Subordinate Lodge or Encampment at the same time; nor shall any Lodge or Encampment confer degrees upon any member of another Lodge or Encampment, without the consent of the Lodge or Encampment to which the member belongs, given under its seal.

ARTICLE XVI.

When a Grand Lodge or Grand Encampment shall have been duly chartered in any State, District, or Territory, all the Lodges and Encampments in said State, District or Territory working under the jurisdiction of the Grand Lodge of the United States, shall thereafter be declared subordinate to, and under the jurisdiction of the Grand Lodge or Encampment of the State, District or Territory in which they are located; and no Lodge or Encampment situated in one State, District, or Territory can be made subordinate to the Grand Lodge or Encampment of another State, District, or Territory.

Article XVII.

No brother, can be admitted to visit, or deposit his card in a Lodge or Encampment out of the State, District, or Territory where he resides, unless he present a card or certificate under the signature of the officers and seal of the Lodge of which he is a member, and signed in the margin, in his own proper hand writing, and prove himself in the T. P. W., and in the Degree in which the Lodge is open. *Provided nevertheless*, a brother may always visit if introduced by a Grand Representative, or other elective officer of the Grand Lodge or Grand Encampment under whose jurisdiction he wishes to visit.

Article XVIII

At each Annual Session the Grand Sire shall appoint in each State, District and Territory, (in which there are not a Grand Lodge and a Grand Encampment,) an officer to be styled " District Deputy Grand Sire," whose duty it shall be to act as the special agent of this Grand Lodge, in relation to the matters herein specified, viz :

1. To act for the Grand Sire, and by his direction to perform whatever may have been ordered to be done by the G. L. of U. S. in the particular District for which the D. D. G. Sire may be appointed.

2. To act as the Representative of this Grand Lodge, and perform all such matters relating to the Order in his District as the Grand Sire shall direct.

3. To obey all special instructions of the Grand Sire in relation to any thing which that officer is required to do for the good of the Order.

4. To act as the agent of the Grand Secretary, and obey the special directions of that officer.

5. To have a general supervision over all Subordinate Lodges and Encampments (in his district) which work under charters granted by the Grand Lodge of the United States.

6. To make semi-annual reports of his acts and doings to the Grand Sire.

7. D. D. G. Sires shall in no case interfere, as officers of this Grand Lodge, with the State Grand Lodges or Encampments.

8. To qualify a brother for the appointment of D. D. G. Sire, he must be a regular contributing member of a Subordinate Lodge and Encampment, and must have attained a rank of P. G. and R. P. D., and in States where Grand Encampments may be established, he must also be a member of such Grand Encampment. The appointment of D. D. Grand Sires shall be made at each annual session, to continue for one year, but they may be revoked for cause during the recess, by the Grand Sire.

Article XIX.

The Representative of each Grand Lodge and Grand Encampment shall be examined by the D. G. Sire as to his qualifications for the office, previous to taking his seat in the Grand Lodge of the United States. On taking his seat he shall be furnished by the Grand Recording Secretary, with a copy of the Constitution, Rules of Order, and Laws of this Grand Lodge. His expenses shall be paid by his Grand Lodge or Encampment, and should he neglect or refuse to attend the meetings of this Lodge when duly notified, he shall be fined five dollars, unless excused by a vote of the Lodge.

Article XX.

Each State, District or Territorial Grand Lodge or Grand Encampment shall furnish its Representative with all documents and papers necessary in the discharge of the duties of his office.

Article XXI.

Each State, District and Territorial Grand Lodge shall annually be furnished with as many copies of the printed proceedings of this Grand Lodge as it has Subordinate Lodges working under its jurisdiction, for its own use; and an equal number to be distributed amongst its Subordinates.

Each Grand Encampment shall be furnished in the same manner. And each Encampment and Lodge working under the warrant of this Grand Lodge shall be furnished with a copy of the proceedings. The Grand Recording Secretary shall see that this law is carried into effect, at as early a date as possible after the close of the annual sessions of this G. Lodge.

ARTICLE XXII.

All dues and moneys for this Grand Lodge shall be paid to the Grand Recording Secretary, and by him be immediately paid over to the Grand Treasurer, who shall give his receipt for the same.

ARTICLE XXIII.

All State, District and Territorial Grand Lodges and Grand Encampments shall enforce upon their Subordinates a strict adherence to the work of the Order, according to the forms furnished by the Grand Lodge of the United States, and shall be held responsible for any irregularities that they may allow under their jurisdiction. They shall neither adopt or use, nor suffer to be adopted or used in their jurisdiction, any other charges, lectures, degrees, ceremonies, forms of installation, or regalia, than those prescribed by the Grand Lodge of the United States.

ARTICLE XXIV.

All Grand and Subordinate Lodges and Encampments under this jurisdiction may at all times open and close their meetings with prayer.

ARTICLE XXV.

The regalia of the Order shall be as follows, to wit:
Aprons and collars of Subordinate Lodges shall be white, trimmed with the emblematic color of the degree intended to be represented, i. e. first degree, white; second degree, pink; third degree, blue; fourth degree, green; fifth degree scarlet; rosettes of the appropriate colors can be worn

on the collars. The Noble Grand shall wear a scarlet collar; Vice Grand, blue collar; Secretary, green collar; Treasurer, green collar; each of which trimmed with white or silver. Supporters of N. G., scarlet sashes; of the V. G., blue sashes; Warden and Conductor, black sashes; Scene Supporters, white sashes; Chaplain, white sash.

The aprons of the elective and appointed officers shall be white, trimmed with the color of the collar or sash indicated for the office.

Past Grands shall wear scarlet collars or sashes, and aprons either white, trimmed with scarlet, or scarlet, trimmed with white. The aprons and collars or sashes of Past Grands may be trimmed with silver lace or fringe, and those having attained to the R. P. Degree may have trimmings of yellow metal. The Grand Officers and Past Grands of Grand Lodges shall wear the regalia of Past Grands, as above defined.

The Encampment regalia shall be black aprons and gloves, and of those Patriarchs who have attained to the R. P. Degree, purple collars, and the aprons and collars trimmed with yellow lace, or fringe.

Regalia for Grand Representatives shall be a collar of purple velvet, not more than four inches in width, with a roll of scarlet velvet. The trimmings to be of yellow metal; the collar to be united in front with three links, to which may be suspended such medal or medals as the member may be entitled to wear.

P. G. Representatives and the Officers and Past Officers of the G. L. of U. S. to wear the regalia above described.

The jewel of the Grand Sire, and P. G. Sire, shall be a medal three inches in diameter of yellow metal, on one side of which shall be the coat of arms of the United States surrounded by an ornament edging of silver.

Representatives and Past Representatives, shall be entitled to wear medals of the size and style above, with the coat of arms of the State represented.—(*Vol. 2, p.* 508, 519,)

Article XXVI.

All expenses of this Grand Lodge shall be paid by an

order drawn on the R. W. Grand Treasurer, signed by the Grand Sire and attested by the Grand Secretary, the same being authorized by a vote of the Grand Lodge.

Article XXVII.

The installation of officers in Subordinate Lodges shall be conducted only in manner and form as provided by the Installation Book.

Article XXVIII.

At the appointed hour, the Grand Sire shall take the chair and organize the meeting by directing the Grand Recording Secretary to call the names of the officers of this Grand Lodge. After which the Secretary shall make report of the number of Representatives present. When, if a quorum be present, the Grand Sire shall call on the Grand Chaplain to address the Supreme Ruler of the Universe in prayer. The Deputy Grand Sire shall then examine the Representatives present, and report to the Grand Sire, and if correct, the Grand Sire shall direct the members to clothe themselves with their regalia and take their seats ; after which the Deputy Grand Sire, at the request of the Grand Sire, shall proclaim the Lodge duly opened. The business of the session shall then be taken up as provided in the Rules of Order; and when the business is concluded, the Grand Chaplain shall offer a prayer and the Deputy Grand Sire shall proclaim the Grand Lodge duly closed.

Article XXIX.

State Grand Lodges are prohibited from conferring the Grand Lodge Degree for a pecuniary consideration, with a view to increasing their revenue, or for any other consideration except the regular performance of the duties of the Noble Grand's chair—the said degree having been designed as a reward for faithful service in the Subordinate Lodges.

Article XXX.

State Grand Lodges and Grand Encampments shall provide laws to protect their brethren in adjoining or distant States, by prohibiting the subordinates under their jurisdiction from initiating persons at places remote from their permanent residence, while Lodges and Encampments are known to be located in the immediate neighborhood.

ARTICLE XXXI.

Past Officers of every description, and members in possession of the Encampment degrees, and all other members of the Order, when visiting Grand or Subordinate Lodges, are entitled to wear the regalia and jewels pertaining to the highest degrees which they may have taken, if they think proper to appear in such regalia.

ARTICLE XXXII.

The T. P. W. is designed only for the use of brethren who are travelling beyond the limits of the jurisdiction, to which they belong; and in order that each brother may be properly instructed in it, and visiting brethren from other jurisdictions properly examined, the two highest elective officers of a Lodge, and the C. P. and S. W. of an Encampment, are to be privately put in possession of the word, at the time of their installation, that they may be qualified either to give or receive it. The Grand Master and Grand Patriarch of a State and their regular Deputies should of course also be in possession of it.

ARTICLE XXXIII.

The fiscal year of this Grand Lodge commences on the first day of July and terminates on the thirtieth of June.

ARTICLE XXXIV.

The charters of all Subordinate Lodges and Encampments, working under the immediate jurisdiction of this Grand Lodge, which fail to make their returns for one year, shall be forfeited, and whenever such remissness occurs, the Grand Sire shall take proper measures to enforce the law.

ARTICLE XXXV.

Any alterations or amendments of these By-Laws must be proposed in writing, at a regular annual communication, and may be considered and acted upon at the same session, but not on the day on which they are offered.

ARTICLE XXXVI.

All former laws and regulations inconsistent with the provisions of these general laws are hereby repealed.

RULES OF ORDER.

1. The presiding officer having taken the chair, the officers and members shall take their respective seats, and at the sound of the gavil there shall be general silence.

2. The business shall be taken up in the following order:—The Grand Lodge shall be opened in due form.

3. The Grand Recording Secretary shall report on certificates of Representatives, which shall be referred to a committee.

4. The minutes of the last annual and intervening meetings shall be read and passed upon.

5. The Grand Sire shall then appoint the following committees, each to consist of three members, viz:—Committee on the State of the Order; Committee on Petitions; Committee on Finance; Committee on Returns and Reports of Grand Lodges and Grand Encampments, and Subordinate Lodges and Encampments; Committee of Correspondence, and Committee on Appeals.

6. The Grand Sire shall also appoint a committee consisting of three members, whose duty it shall be to take in charge, and prepare for the action of the Grand Lodge, all business appertaining to State Grand Lodges or Grand Encampments, which shall not be represented by the personal attendance of delegates.

7. The report of the Grand Sire as to his acts and doings during the recess of this Grand Lodge shall be presented.

8. Annual reports of the Grand Corresponding Secretary and Grand Treasurer shall be presented.

9. Petitions shall be presented, read and referred.

10. Other communications shall be presented and read.

11. The above order of business may be dispensed with at the discretion of the Lodge.

12. Election and installation of officers for the ensuing term shall take place on the second day of the session.

13. During the sitting of the Grand Lodge, each Representative or visiter, on entering or leaving the Lodge, shall address the presiding officer with the sign of the R. P. Degree.

14. No motion shall be subject to debate until it shall have been seconded, and stated by the Chair—it shall be reduced to writing at the request of any member.

15. When a question is before the Lodge, no motion shall be received unless it be to adjourn, to refer, the previous question, to lay on the table, to postpone indefinitely, to postpone to a certain time, or to amend; and the motions just enumerated shall take precedence in the order of enumeration. The first four shall be decided without debate.

16. On a call of Representatives of three States, Districts or Territories, a majority of the Lodge may demand that the previous question shall be put, which shall always be in this form : " *Shall the main question be now put ?*" and until it be decided, it shall preclude all amendments and all further debate.

17. When the reading of any paper or other matter is called for and the same is objected to by any member, it shall be determined by vote of the Lodge, without debate.

18. Before putting a question, the presiding officer shall ask, " Is the Lodge ready for the question?" If no member rise to speak, he shall rise and put it. While the presiding officer is putting a question, or addressing the Lodge, none shall walk out of, or across the room, or entertain private discourse ; and after he shall have risen to put it, no member shall speak upon it.

19. The presiding officer, or any member doubting the decision of a question, may call for a division of the Lodge.

20. No member shall be permitted to speak or vote, unless clothed in regalia, according to his rank and station, and occupying his seat at the place designated for him.

21. In the election of officers, the Grand Sire shall put the question of the nomination of Grand Sire, and the election shall proceed before the nomination of Deputy Grand Sire, and so with the other officers. During the progress of a ballot for an officer, no motion can be entertained, or debate or explanation permitted.

22. Every officer and member shall be designated by his proper title or office, according to his standing in the Order.

23. Every member, when he speaks or offers a motion shall rise and respectfully address the presiding officer; and while speaking he shall confine himself to the question in debate, avoiding all personalities and indecorous language, as well as all reflections upon the Lodge, or any of its members.

24. Should two members rise to speak at the same time, the chair shall decide which is entitled to the floor. And no member shall interrupt or disturb another while speaking, unless to call him to order for words spoken

25. If a member while speaking, shall be called to order, he shall, at the request of the Chair, take his seat until the question of order is determined, when if permitted he may proceed again.

26. The decisions of the Chair on points of order, may be appealed from by any member, and in such cases the question shall be, " Shall the decision of the Chair stand as the judgement of the Lodge?"

27. No member shall speak more than twice on the same question, until all the members wishing to speak have had an opportunity to do so.

28. When any petition, memorial or communication is presented, a brief statement of its contents shall be made by the introducer or the Chair. And after it has been read,

a brief notice of its purport shall be entered upon the journal.

29.   When a blank is to be filled, the question shall be · taken first upon the highest sum or number, and the longest or latest time proposed.

30. Any member may call for a division of a question when the sense will admit.

31. When one-fifth of the members rise in favor of taking a question by Yeas and Nays, they shall be ordered and recorded.

32. The vote by States may be called on any question, if required by two States.

33. All committees shall be appointed by the Chair, unless otherwise ordered.

34. Any member who voted with the majority may call for a re-consideration of a vote, at the same session in which it was passed, and if sustained by a majority of all the votes, the re-consideration shall be carried.

35. No matter shall be considered at each morning session of the Grand Lodge until all reports of committees are gone through with, and the Grand Sire shall call for the reports of committees in the order of their appointment.

36. A committee appointed at one session to perform a duty, are bound to report, although some of the members of the committee have ceased to be members of this body. —(*Vol.* 2, *p.* 29.)

37. The previous question cuts off all amendments.—(*Vol.* 2, *p.* 205-6, 213.)

38. Any member has a right to protest, and to have his protest spread upon the journal.—(*Vol.* 1, *p.* 81, 139, *vol.* 2, *p.* 130.)

39. A representative whose seat is disputed, may nevertheless offer a resolution.—(*Vol.* 1, *p.* 90.)

40. The Grand Sire is entitled to the casting vote at an election of officers.—(*Vol.* 1, *p.* 32.)

41. The previous question may be called, though no amendment be pending at the time.—(*Journal passim.*)

42. Every member is bound to vote, serve on committees, and accept nominations unless excused by vote.—(*Journal passim.*)

APPENDIX II.

FORMS.

~~~~~~~~~~~~~~~~~

No. 1.

Diploma.

We, the Most Worthy Grand Sire, Right Worthy Deputy Grand Sire, Officers and Members of the Grand Lodge of the Independent Order of Odd-Fellows of the United States of America and jurisdiction thereunto belonging:

Do hereby certify, that our well beloved brother   is a member of   under the jurisdiction of the Grand   and that he is a true and worthy member of our Order.

In testimony whereof we grant him this certificate, and recommend him to the friendship of all the brethren of the Independent Order of Odd Fellows throughout the globe. And that the same may not be of use to any other person, we have caused him in our presence to sign his name in the margin.

<div align="right">

G. S.

D. G S.

</div>

G. C. and R. S.

~~~~~~~~~~~

No. 2.

Representative's Diploma.

We, the Most Worthy Grand Sire, Right Worthy Deputy Grand Sire, Officers and Members of the Grand Lodge of the Independent Order of Odd-Fellows of the United States of America and jurisdiction thereunto belonging.

In Grand Lodge assembled, present a Representation from Maryland, New York, Pennsylvania, District of Columbia, Ohio, Louisiana, New Jersey, Kentucky, Virginia, Connecticut, Massachusetts, New Hampshire, Maine, South Carolina, Missouri, Georgia, Alabama, Michigan, Tennessee, Indiana, Wisconsin, North Carolina, Mississippi, Illinois and Delaware, have unanimously presented to a well

beloved brother   the R. W.
G. Representative of the Grand Lodge of   this
Diploma, as an evidence of his regular communion and fellowship
with the Independent Order of Odd-Fellows, and in appreciation of
his zeal and devotion to the welfare of our beloved Order.

 Done at the City of Baltimore, on the   day of   in
the year of our Order in the United States,   and of our Lord, 18

                                                        G. M.
                                                        G. S.

              G. C. and R. S.

              ~~~~~~~~~~~~~

                   No. 3.

        Certificate of Grand Representative

                 F. L. and T.
To the R. W. Grand Lodge of the United States, of the I. O. of O. F.
    THIS CERTIFIES, That P. G.
has been duly elected, (or appointed,) Representative from the Grand
Lodge, (or Grand Encampment) of
to the Grand Lodge of the United States.
    Witness our hands and seal of the Grand
              this   day of

                        G. MASTER, (or G. PATRIARCH.)
                        G. SECRETARY, (or G. SCRIBE.)

              ~~~~~~~~~~~~~

                   No. 4.

     Petition for a Warrant of a Subordinate Lodge.

To the Grand Sire, Officers and Members
          of the Grand Lodge of the United States:
    The Petition of the undersigned, holding withdrawal Cards from
Lodges legally recognized by your R. W. Body, respectfully represents, that it would be consistent with the advantage of the Order, to
establish a Subordinate Lodge, to be located at   in the State of
    Wherefore your Petitioners pray, that a Warrant may duly issue
in pursuance of the Laws of your R. W. Body.
          Dated at   this   day of

No 5

Petition for a Warrant of a Subordinate Encampment.

To the Grand Sire Officers and Members
of the Grand Lodge of the United States.

The Petition of the undersigned Patriarchs, holding withdrawal Cards, from legal Encampments, (or instructed in the Encampment Degrees, under commission of the Grand Sire,) respectfully represents, that it would be consistent with the advantage of the Order, to establish a Subordinate Encampment; to be located at   in the State of

Wherefore, your Petitioners pray that a Warrant may duly issue in pursuance of the Laws of the R. W. Body.

Dated at   this   day of

No. 6.

Petition for a Grand Lodge or Grand Encampment.

To the Grand Sire, Officers and Members of the
Grand Lodge of the United States, I. O O. F.

The petition of   Lodge, (or Encampment,) No.
No.   No   of   respectfully represent that at present they work under warrants granted by your honorable body, that the Order has increased in the   and at present they have   Past Grands, (or Past C. Patriarchs,) in good standing They are of the opinion that it would be of advantage to the Order, that a Grand Lodge (or Grand Encampment) should be established in the
They therefore pray your honorable Lodge to grant a charter for a Grand Lodge (or Grand Encampment) in the State of   to be located at

Witness our hands and seals this   day of

A. B, Representative of No
C D, Representative of No.
E F, Representative of No.

No. 7.

Warrant for Lodge or Encampment.
I. O. O F

To all whom it may concern:

i,   Most Worthy Grand Sire of the Grand Lodge of the

Independent Order of Odd-Fellows, of the United States of North America, and the jurisdiction of the Order thereunto belonging:—

FRIENDSHIP, LOVE, TRUTH.

Know ye, that by virtue of the powers in me vested, I do hereby authorise and empower our trusty and well beloved brethren

their successors duly and legally elected, to constitue a   in the

      of   and State of   to be known

and hailed by the title of   .

And I do further authorise and empower our said trusty and well beloved brethren and their successors, to admit and make Odd-Fellows according to the ancient usages and customs of the Order, and not contrarywise; with full power and authority to hear and determine all and singular, matters and things relating to the Order within the jurisdiction of the said   according to the rules and regulations of the Grand Lodge of the United States. Provided always, that the said above named brethren, and their successors, pay due respect to the Grand Lodge of the United States, and the ordinances thereof, otherwise this Dispensation to be of no force or effect.

Given under my hand, and Seal of the Grand Lodge of the United States, at the City of Baltimore, in the State of Maryland, this   day of

[SEAL.]   By the Grand Sire.

        R. and C S.

No. 8.

Form of Warrant for Grand Lodge or Grand Encampment.

I. O. O. F.

To all whom it may concern.

I   Most Worthy Grand Sire of the Grand Lodge of the Indepedent Order of Odd-Fellows, of the United States of North America, and the jurisdiction of the Order thereunto belonging:

FRIENDSHIP, LOVE, TRUTH.

Know ye, that by virtue of the powers in me vested, I do hereby authorise and empower our trusty and well beloved   to constitute a   in the   of   and State of   to be known and hailed by the title of   .

And I do further authorise and empower our said trusty and well beloved to hear and determine all and singular, matters and things relating to the Order within the jurisdiction of the said according to the rules and regulations of the Grand Lodge of the United States. Provided always, that the said pays due respect to the Grand Lodge of the United States, and the ordinances thereof; and provided also, this Dispensation shall be approved at the next session of the said Grand Lodge of the United States, otherwise to be of no force or effect.

Given under my hand, and Seal of the Grand Lodge of the United States, at the City of Baltimore, in the State of Maryland, this day of and of our Order the

[SEAL.]

Grand Sire.

C. S.

~~~~~~

No. 9.

Commission to open Lodge or Encampment.

I O. O. F.

I. Most Worthy Grand Sire of the Independent Order of Odd-Fellows, in and for the United States of North America, and the jurisdiction of the Order thereunto belonging:—

To our Worthy Brother, Greeting:

Reposing special confidence in your zeal and ability, I do, by virtue of the powers and authorities in me vested, hereby authorise and empower you to call to your assistance a sufficient number of known, approved, and duly qualified in the of and State of to open and constitute a new to be held there,—and to proceed to the installation of our Worthy Brother who shall be elected and other the Officers of a new there to be established and constituted,—to be hailed and known by the title of according to the most ancient and honorable custom of the Order, and not contrarywise,—and make report to me hereunto annexed of your proceedings.

This Dispensation to remain in full force for three months from the date hereof, and no longer.

Given under my hand and seal, at the   in the

on   this   day of

[SEAL]

By the Grand Sire.

R and C. S.

~~~~~~

No. 10

Commission to confer Encompment Degrees

I O. of O. F

Whereas,   residing at the   of   have by petition requested to be enabled to open an Encampment of Patriarchs at the place aforenamed; and have produced to me sufficient testimony of their regular connection in the Order:

Therefore, I,   Most Worthy Grand Sire of the Independent Order of Odd-Fellows, in and for the United States of America, and the jurisdiction thereunto belonging; by virtue of the powers and authorities in me vested, do by these presents hereby authorise and empower our worthy and well beloved Patriarch   in whom I repose special confidence, to call to his aid such number of known, approved and duly qualified Patriarchs as may be disposed to assist in the   of   and   of   and there to initiate the above named brethren into the mysteries of the Encampment Branch of the Order, conferring upon them the several degrees thereunto appertaining, according to the most ancient and honorable custom of our Order, and not contrarywise so as to enable said Brethren to make petition in due and lawful form as Patriarchs of the Order for a charter for an Encampment to be located in said

And the said Patriarch to whom this commission is entrusted, is hereby required to make full and immediate report to me, of his proceedings.

This Dispensation to remain in force for three months from the date hereof, and no longer.

Given under my hand, and the Seal of the Grand Lodge of the United States, at the   of   in the
of   this   day of

[SEAL.]

By the Grand Sire.

C. and R. S.

No. 11.

[Form of Dispensation to continue operations where a Charter has been destroyed.]

I. O. O. F.

I,   Most Worthy Grand Sire of the Independent Order of Odd-Fellows, in and for the Uunited States of North America, and the jurisdiction of the Order thereunto belonging:

To the   of   No.   held in the   or   in the State of   these Presents in

FRIENDSHIP, LOVE AND TRUTH, *Come Greeting.*

Whereas, it has been represented to me that the   of your has been destroyed by   and sufficient proof has been given that there is no illegal concealment nor wilful destruction of the same.

Now therefore, by virtue of the powers and authorities in me vested, I do hereby authorise, empower and request you, the present and succeeding   officers and members of the said   No. to continue your labors in the same full and complete manner to all intents and purposes as you could or might legally have done if your said   had not been destroyed, and was still in existence agreeably to all the usages, rules and regulations of Odd-Fellowship and especially to those of our Most Worthy Grand Lodge of the United States, and not contrarywise.

This dispensation to continue in force until the next Annual Communication of our said Most Worthy Grand Lodge, and until its pleasure in the premises shall have been made known to you.

Given under my hand and seal, at the   or   in the or   this   day or   in

[SEAL.]

By the Grand Sire.

C. and R. S.

No. 12.

Commission for District Deputy Grand Sire.

I. O. O. F.

FRIENDSHIP, LOVE AND TRUTH.

I,   Most Worthy Grand Sire of the I. O. of O. F.
of the United States and the jurisdiction thereunto belonging, to our
well beloved brother   and to all whom it may concern,
send greeting.

Know ye, that reposing special confidence in your knowledge and
discretion, I do by virtue of the power and authority in me vested,
hereby appoint and commission you the said   our District
Deputy for the   of   to be entitled,
Worthy District Deputy Grand Sire of the I. O. of O. F. of the United
States, for the   of   .

And as our District Deputy Grand Sire for said   you are
empowered and directed to act as the Special Agent of the Grand
Lodge of the United States, in relation to the matters herein specified, viz.

To act for the Grand Sire, and by his directions to do and perform
whatever may have been ordered to be done and performed by the.
Grand Lodge of the United States in your

To act as the Representative of the Grand Lodge of the United
States, and do and perform all such matters relating to the Order in
your   as the Grand Sire shall direct. You shall
obey all special instructions of the Grand Sire, in relation to any thing
which that Officer is required to do for the "Good of the Order."

You are to act as the Agent of the Grand Secretary, and obey the
special directions of that Officer.

You are to have the general supervision over all Subordinate.
Lodges and Encampments in your   which work under
Charters granted by the Grand Lodge of the United States.   •

It is your duty to see that the Work of the Order is performed
uniformly by such Subordinates; to install or cause to be installed by
a P G. or P. C. P., in regular form, at the periods designated by the
regulations of the Grand Lodge of the United States, the Officers duly
elected and appointed in the several Subordinates in your jurisdiction;
to confer the Past Official Degrees on Past Officers, upon the presentation of proper certificates from their respective   ; to

make reports during the months in which installations take place—of the Officers installed—and the amount of dues from each subordinate, to the Grand Lodge of the United States. And to make, to the office of the G. Secretary, a full report during the month of July in each year, of your acts and doings, and of the work, condition and prospects of the Order in your

You are required to make Semi-Annual reports of your acting and doings to the Grand Sire.

You are in no case to interfere, as an Officer of the Grand Lodge of the United States, with Grand Lodges or Encampments.

This Dispensation shall go into effect from the day of the date hereof, and remain in full force for and during the period of year unless sooner revoked by the Grand Sire.

In testimony whereof, I have hereunto set my hand and affixed the seal of the Grand Lodge of the United States, this   day of

By the Grand Sire,

G. C. Sec'ry.

No. 13.

Visiting Card.

Friendship, Love, and Truth.
INDEPENDENT ORDER OF ODD FELLOWS.

To all whom it may concern:

This Certifies, that   whose name is written on the margin of this card in his own proper hand writing, is a member in good standing of   No.   held at, and working under a Charter duly granted by authority of the Right Worthy Grand   of the State of   We therefore recommend him to your Friendship and Protection, and admission into all regular   of Odd-Fellows, for the space of   from the date, and no longer.

In Witness whereof, we have subscribed our names and affixed the Seal of our   this   day o. in the year of our Lord one thousand eight hundred and

[SEAL.]

8*

No. 14.

Withdrawal Card.

Friendship, Love, and Truth.

INDEPENDENT ORDER OF ODD-FELLOWS.

To all whom it may concern

This certifies that our well beloved Brother
whose signature, written by himself, is properly situated on the
margin of this card, was regular admitted a Member of our
by   on the   day of   18   and has paid all
demands against him up to this day, and is under no charge whatever. We therefore recommend him to your Friendship and Protection, and admission into any regular   of Odd-Fellows,
to which he may apply within one year from the date hereof.

This Card is granted by   No.   which was duly
instituted at   on the   day or   18   by authority
of the Right Worthy Grand   of the State of   .

In witness whereof, we subscribe hereto our hands, and affix the
Seal of our   this   day of   in the Year
of our Lord One Thousand Eight Hundred and

[SEAL.]

~~~~~~~~~

No. 15.

Form of Card presented to Wife or Widow of an Odd-Fellow.

Friendship, Love, and Truth.

INDEPENDENT ORDER OF ODD-FELLOWS.

To all to whom these presents shall come:—Greeting:

This Certifies, that   whose name is endorsed on the
margin of this Card in her own proper hand writing, is the wife of
our well beloved Brother who (is) a member of Lodge, No.   held
at   and working under authority of a Charter duly granted
by authority of the Right Worthy Grand Lodge of the
We therefore recommend her to your Friendship and Protection
wherever she may be, throughout the world,—for the space of
and no longer.

In Witness whereof, we have subscribed our names and affixed
the Seal of our Lodge, this   day or
in the year

N. G.

V. G.

SEC'RY.

No. 16

Form of Funeral Procession and Regalia.

1. *Resolved*, That the Regalia to be worn by all brothers of the Order, when attending the funeral of a deceased brother, be as follows:

A black crape rosette, having a centre of the color of the highest Degree to which the wearer may have attained, to be worn on the left breast; above it a sprig of evergreen, and below it (if the wearer be an Elective or Past Officer) the jewel or jewels which as such he may be entitled to wear.

2. *Resolved*, That the ordinary mourning badge to be worn by brothers in memory of a deceased brother, be a strip of black crape passed through one buttonhole only of the left lapel of the coat, and tied with a narrow ribbon of the color of the highest Degree to which the wearer may have attained.

3. *Resolved*, That the order of procedure at the funeral of a deceased brother, be as follows:

At the appointed hour the Subordinate Lodge of which such brother was a member, shall meet at its Lodge room, and shall open in the Initiatory Degree; and the N. G. shall appoint a marshal and such number of assistant marshals as may be required. The Lodge shall thereupon close, and the brothers shall pass in procession from the Lodge room to the place from which the funeral may have been appointed to start, in the following order:

1. The marshal, wearing a black scarf, and bearing a baton bound with a band of black crape.

2. The O. G. bearing a red staff in like mourning.

3. The Scene Supporters bearing white wands in like mourning.

4. Members of the Initiatory Degree, in order of juniority, two abreast.

5. Members of the White, Pink, Royal Blue, Green and Scarlet Degrees, respectively, in like order.

6. Members of the Lodge having the Patriarchal, G. R. and R. P. Degrees, respectively, in like order.

7. The I. G., bearing the regalia and insignia indicative of the rank in the Order of the deceased brother.

8. The Treasurer, Assistant, Permanent or Financial Secretary or Secretaries, and the Secretary of the Lodge.

9. The P G., supported by his R and L Supporters, each bearing his wand of office, bound with a band of black crape

10. The Chaplain, wearing a white scarf, and supported by the Warden and Conductor, each bearing his staff of office in like mourning

11. The N. G , supported by his R. and L Supporters, each bearing his wand of office in like mourning.

12. The Past Grands of the Lodge, in order of juniority.

13 Brethren of invited Lodges, those of each Lodge arranged in the order above prescribed; the Lodges, when more than one may be represented, arranged in order of juniority.

On arriving at the place appointed for the starting of the funeral, the brothers shall take position in the above order immediately before the corpse, and shall precede it to the place of interment.

On arriving at such place of interment, the brothers shall open to the right and left, and allow the corpse, mourners, &c, to pass through, the brothers on either side standing uncovered, the hat held in the left hand of each, and joining hands with each other. And after the passing of the corpse, mourners, &c , between the two lines, the brothers shall re-form in procession after them in reversed order, and close the procession into and within the place of interment.

After the performance of such religious service as the friends of the deceased may cause to be there performed, and before the final closing of the grave, the brothers shall form silently, and as nearly as may be according to the order above set forth, uncovered, the hat in the left hand of each, and joining hands with each other, in one or more circles, as regular as the nature of the ground may admit. around the grave; when the Chaplain, or in default of a Chaplain, the N. G may address the brothers and offer up a prayer, or may address the brothers without the offering of a prayer; and after such address or prayer, or both, or if there be no address or prayer, then after a pause suited to the solemnity of the occasion, the N. G. shall advance singly to the head of the grave, and cast into it with the right hand the sprig of evergreen from his regalia, and shall return to his place; whereupon the brothers from left to right in regular succession, and in such numbers at a time as not to cause confusion, shall advance to the grave, shall cast into it (each with the right hand) the sprig of evergreen from their regalia, and shall return to their place. And after all have done this, and the grave shall have been filled up or closed, the brothers shall silently re-form into procession according to the order observed in coming to the place of interment, and shall return in such order to the Lodge room, where the N. G., shall declare the funeral ceremonies to be closed.

4. *Resolved,* That if at the time of his death the deceased brother was a member of an Encampment, or of a State, District, or Territorial Grand Lodge, or Grand Encampment, or of the Grand Lodge of the United States, the Chaplain and highest Officer or Officers present, of such Encampment, or Grand Body or Bodies, supported each by two members thereof, shall take position in the funeral procession next after the Chaplain and N. G., respectively, of the Subordinate Lodge of the deceased, and shall take precedence of such N. G., and of each other, according to their respective rank, in conducting the ceremony of interment as above set forth.

5. *Resolved,* That in other processions of the Order the rules of precedence above set forth, so far as they may admit of being followed, shall be adhered to.

FUNERAL SERVICE.

We are assembled, my brethren, to render the last office which the living may minister to the dead.

Man is born to die. The coffin, the grave, the sepulchre, speak to us in language that cannot be misunderstood, however unheeded it may be, of " man's latter end." Youth in its harmlessness and comparative innocency, and manhood with its wonted vigor and pride of strength are not more exempt than decrepid and tottering age from the fixed law of being, which dedicates all that is mortal to decay and death.

This truth is inscribed in the great volume of nature upon its every page. The beautiful and the sublime which the handiwork of the Creator displays on our every side, fearfully associate the unerring certainty of the end of all things, amid the vividness of the moral which they are ever suggesting to the contemplative mind.

Day after day, we are called upon to follow our fellow creatures to that bourne whence no traveller returns: but from the house of mourning we go forth again to mingle in the crowded world, heedless perhaps of the precarious tenure of life and the certainty of that end to which all flesh is rapidly tending. He who gives the vigour of body, without warning, paralizes the stout heart, and strikes down the athletic frame—the living of to-day, become the dead of the morrow.

Men appear upon and disappear from the stage of life, as wave meets wave and parts upon the troubled waters—"In the midst of life we are in death." He, whose lips now echo these tones of solemn warning, in turn will be stilled in the cold and cheerless house of the dead, and in the Providence of God none may escape.

Let us then so far improve the lesson as to be prepared for that change, which leads to life eternal.

PRAYER.

Our Father and our God, who art the resurrection and the life; in whom whosoever believeth shall live though he die; and whosoever liveth and believeth in thee shall not die—hear, we beseech thee, the voice of thy creatures here assembled, and turn not away from our supplications.

We humbly beseech Thee, so to imbue us with a conviction of our entire helplessness and dependence upon thee, that we may be brought to meditate upon the uncertainty of life and the certainty of death. In the dispensation of thy Providence, thou hast summoned from amongst us our brother, and we the surviving monuments of thy mercy are gathered together to commit his remains to the earth.— Give, O God, we beseech thee, thy Holy Spirit to us, whom thou hast spared; increase our knowledge, and confirm our faith in thee, for ever.

[Bless and comfort, we pray thee, those whom it has pleased thee to add to the number of the disconsolate; buoy them up under this heavy stroke, sustain them against despondency. O! wilt thou be their Father and their God, and pour down from on high thy blessings upon their heads.] Bless, O Heavenly Father! the brethren here assembled, imbue them with the wisdom of thy laws, and draw them unto thee by the cords of thy inestimable love; impress them with their duty to each other as brethren, and their obligations in the various relations of human life, and finally, bless our beloved Order throughout the globe. Preserve its principles and its purposes from innovation; sustain it from the shafts of enmity—protect it from self-immolation, and shield it from all evil, and unto thee we shall render the praise, forever—AMEN.

The Form of Prayer adopted with Funeral Address and the Ceremony is left optional with Lodges or Encampments, whether they use it or none,—the form prescribed to be used if any.

Report of the R. W. Grand Lodge of the State of ——, I. O. O. F., to the R. W. Grand Lodge of the United States, commencing ——, 18—, and ending ——, 18—.

The R. W. Grand Lodge of —— is composed of —— members, and has under its jurisdiction —— working Lodges.

LODGES.	Numbers.	Where held.	County.	Time of Meeting.	Initiations.	Rejections.	Admitted by Card.	Withdrawn by Card.	Reinstatements.	Suspensions.	Expulsions.	Deaths.	Past Grands.	Contributing Members.	Names of Past Grand Masters.	Revenue.	REMARKS.
																⊕	
																⊕	

In witness whereof, we have hereunto set our hands, and the Seal of the Grand Lodge of the State of —— this —— day of ——, A. D. 18—.

A—— B——, G. Master:
C—— D——, G. Secretary

[L. S.]

☞ The names of brothers suspended, for causes other than non-payment of dues; and the names of expelled members, and the cause of expulsion shall be appended, and attested under the hands of the Grand Master and Grand Secretary, together with the Seal of the Grand Lodge.

Annual Report of Relief of the Subordinate Lodges under the jurisdiction of the R. W. Grand Lodge of the State of —— I. O. O. F., showing the relief in the year commencing ——, 18—, and ending —— 18—.

LODGES.	Numbers.	No. of brothers relieved.	No. of wid. fam. relieved.	No. of brothers buried.	Amount paid for relief of brothers.	Amount paid for relief of widowed families.	Amount paid for education of orphans.	Amount paid for burying the dead.	Total Amount.	REMARKS.
					$	$	$	$	$	
					$	$	$	$	$	

In witness whereof, we have hereunto set our hands and the seal of the Grand Lodge of the State of ——, this — day of—, A D. 18—.

A—— B——, G. Master.

C—— D——, G. Secretary.

[L. S.]

Semi-Annual Report of ——— Lodge, No. —, of the State of ———, to the R. W. Grand Lodge of the United States, I. O. O. F., for the term ending ———.

	Names of persons initiated.
	Names of brothers admitted by Card.
	Names of applicants rejected.
	Names of brothers withdrawn.
	Names of brothers suspended.
	Cause of suspension.
	Names of brothers expelled.
	Cause of expulsion.
	Names of brothers reinstated.
	Names of brothers deceased.

SUMMARY.

- Initiated,
- Admitted by Card,
- Rejected,
- Withdrawn,
- Suspended,
- Expelled,
- Deceased,
- Reinstated,
- Degrees conferred,
- Members in good standing,
- Elective officers for the ensuing quarter,

N G
V G
S
T
P S

RECEIPTS.

	Dollars.	Cents.
Contributions,		
Initiations,		
Admissions,		
Cards, &c.,		
Degrees,		
Total,		
Per centage due R. W. Grand Lodge, U. S.		

[L. S.]

ATTEST.

N. G.
V. G.

[L. 9.]

Semi-Annual Report of ——— Encampment, No. ——, of the State of ———, to the R. W. Grand Lodge, of the United States, I. O. O. F., for the term ending ———.

Names of brothers initiated.	
Names of Patriarchs excelled.	
Names of Patriarhs admitted by card.	
Names of applicants rejected.	
Names of Patr'chs withdrawn.	
Names of Patr'chs suspended.	
Cause of suspension.	
Names of Patr'chs expelled.	
Cause of expulsion.	
Names of Patr'chs reinstated.	
Names of Patr'chs deceased.	

SUMMARY.

Initiated, - - -
Admitted oy Card, - -
Rejected, - - -
Withdrawn, - - -
Suspended, - - -
Expelled, - - -
Reinstated, - - -
Deceased, - - -
Degrees conferred, - -
Members in good standing, -
Elective officers for the ensuing quarter, - - -

N G
V G
S
T
P S

RECEIPTS.

	Dollars	Cents.
Contributions,		
Initiations,		
Admissions.		
Cards,		
Degrees,		
Total,		
Per centage due R. W. Grand Lodge, U. S.		

C. P
H. P
Scribe

Report of the R. W. Grand Encampment of the State of —, I. O. O. F., to the R. W. G. Lodge of the United States, commencing —, 18—, and ending —, 18—.

The R. W. G. Encampment of — is composed of — members, and has under its jurisdiction — working Lodges

ENCAMPMENTS.	Numbers.	Where held.	County.	Time of Meeting.	Initiations.	Rejections.	Admitted by Card.	Withdrawn by Card.	Reinstatements.	Suspensions and cause other than for non-payment of dues.	Expulsions and cause.	Deaths.	Past Chief Patriarchs.	Past High Priests.	Contributing Patriarchs	Names of P. G. P's.	Revenue.	REMARKS.
																	⊕	

FORMS.

In witness whereof, we have hereunto set our hands, and the Seal of the Grand Encampment of the State of — this — day of —, A. D 18—.

[L. s.]

A—— B——, G. Patriarch.
C—— D——, G. Scribe.

Annual Report of Relief of the Subordinate Encampments under the ju risdiction of the R. W. Grand Lodge of the State of —— I. O. O. F., showing the relief in the year commencing —, 18—, and ending — 18—.

ENCAMPMENTS.	Numbers.	No. of Patriarchs relieved.	No. of wid. fam. relieved.	No. of Patriarhs buried.	Amount paid for relief of Patriarchs.	Amount paid for relief of widowed families.	Amount paid for education of orphans.	Amount paid for burying the dead.	Total Amount	REMARKS.
					$	$	$	$	$	
					$	$	$	$	$	

In witness whereof, we have hereunto set our hands and the seal of the Grand Encampment of the State of ——, this — day of—, A. D. 18—.

A—— B——, G. Patriarch.

C— D——, G. Scribe.

[L. S.]